THE PRIMETIME PRESIDENCY OF RONALD REAGAN

The Era of the Television Presidency

ROBERT E. DENTON, JR.

D0068968

PRAEGER

New York
Westport, Connecticut
London

Library of Congress Cataloging-in-Publication Data

Denton, Robert E., Jr.
  The primetime presidency of Ronald Reagan : the era of the
television presidency / Robert E. Denton, Jr.
    p. cm.
  Bibliography: p.
  Includes index.
  ISBN 0-275-92603-6 (alk. paper)
    1. Presidents—United States. 2. Communication in politics—
United States. 3. Television in politics—United States.
4. Reagan, Ronald.   I. Title.
JK518.D453   1988
353.03'23'0924—dc19   88-5910

Library of Congress Catalog Card Number: 88-5910
ISBN: 0-275-92603-6

First published in 1988

Praeger Publishers, One Madison Avenue, New York, NY 10010
A division of Greenwood Press, Inc.

Printed in the United States of America

The paper used in this book complies with the
Permanent Paper Standard issued by the National
Information Standards Organization (Z39.48-1984).

10 9 8 7 6 5 4 3 2 1

This book is dedicated to my wife Paula,
the star of my primetime.

"Modern politics requires mastery of television. I think you know I've never warmed up to television, and it's never warmed up to me. I like to look people in the eye. There's something about television I've never been comfortable with."

Walter Mondale, November 7, 1984. Press conference the morning after the election in which Ronald Reagan received 59 percent of the popular vote—more votes than ever received by a United States presidential candidate.

Contents

Preface

This book is more about the institutional United States presidency than about Ronald Reagan. The core argument is obvious and simple but the consequences determine who runs for president and who is elected, and impacts the very nature of U.S. democracy. Since the 1970s, with the decline of political parties, people have turned to the media for information and guidance in selecting their presidents. Television became the primary means of getting to know the issues and candidates. It also, vicariously, allowed us to challenge candidates or presidents and keep them honest. The power of the media was thought to be in the hands of a few "northeastern liberal elites." But soon candidates began to surround themselves with communication professionals and consultants whose job was to ensure that the candidate's message and image prevailed. Of course, once elected, presidents need such professionals more than ever. With Reagan, the media elites were helpless to expose his lack of "substance" or make issues out of obvious gaffes. The messenger became the message—molded and shaped to fit the requirements of television.

Television has become the primary medium and tool of both campaigning and governing. As a result, the nature of the contemporary presidency is directly linked to the evolution of television. The Reagan revolution is not so much in ideology or programs but in instituting the prime-time presidency. There are three critical dimensions to the primetime presidency. First, the message must fit the medium in both form and content. Second, industry demands for news must be carefully crafted by the incumbent. Finally, today's president must be, if not an actor, at least a "media celebrity."

Ronald Reagan is our first true television president. His persona, messages, and behavior fit the medium's requirements in terms of form, content, and industry demands. Reagan made television the instrument of governing. His presidency provides the blueprint for public esteem and popularity.

In the future, products of the media will become the primary source of potential presidential candidates. It is too expensive to generate name recognition. Those who already have it clearly have an advantage. Because of the intimate nature of television, personal characteristics of candidates are more important than issues. Those who win the presidency are those who fulfill the role expectations of the office, which have little to do with policy formation or execution. Because of the nature of the medium, presidents use the medium to confirm rather than challenge, to present rather than to engage the public. National audiences require generic appeals and predictable responses. Presidential leadership today is charismatic rather than programmatic. We see our presidents more but know them less. Primarily because of television, presidents and presidential candidates will increasingly look the same, sound the same, and, unfortunately, act the same. The presidency has become a product, and the consumers were ready for Reagan's brand above all others.

Television was going to make us more politically informed and democratic. The fact is that television has not made us more informed in our electoral choices or more democratic in terms of electoral participation. And, as the Reagan presidency has demonstrated, television cannot serve as a check on presidential power. Media orchestration by an administration can dominate news coverage and presentation.

Chapter 1 addresses the notion of Ronald Reagan as "the Great Communicator" by looking at the changing nature of political rhetoric and suggests three explanations for Reagan's rhetorical successes. Chapter 2 provides a broad discussion of the mass media and the presidency by focusing on the social power of the media, media and politics, and media and campaigns. This chapter provides a theoretical perspective and review of the literature on the role of the mass media in contemporary politics. The focus of Chapter 3 is on the role of television in presidential politics. The chapter discusses the nature of television as a communication medium and its specific impact upon contemporary political information, participation, and presidential governing. The primetime presidency of Ronald Reagan is defined and detailed in Chapter 4. Dimensions of Reagan's television personality and how the medium became the message provide the basis of discussion and analysis. Finally, Chapter 5 investigates the future of the presidency in the age of television.

Although this is a descriptive media study, the bias is clearly institutional and rhetorical. The presidency is primarily and essentially a rhetorical institution. It is defined by public communication and functions through communication in a variety of ways and contexts. Much has been written about individual presidents, less about the institutional presidency. The focus of my research for several years has been to investigate three levels of interaction involving the presidency:

1. The interaction of the office with the general public, which includes considerations of campaigns and the generating and sustaining of public support.
2. The interaction of the office with specific individuals, which includes considerations of presidential myth, persona, and role expectations.
3. The interaction of the office with officeholders, which includes considerations of how individuals adapt to and adopt the historical, symbolic, and mythical qualities of the office.

My general methodological orientation is dramatism or symbolic interactionism. Within this framework I conduct microscopic analyses to usually discover, confirm, or deny an institutional phenomenon. Such an approach, at least for me, has resulted in the following broad generalizations:

1. The institution of the U.S. presidency is greater than any individual. The office greatly influences the officeholder, who must confront already established expectations of presidential performance and behavior.
2. The set of expected presidential roles results from the interaction of the office with the public. The role sets are created, sustained, and permeated

through interaction comprised of campaigns, socialization, history, and myth.

3. There is a clear, rather systematic process of transformation from candidate to president where the candidate must confront the "political self" and the public definition of the presidential role. Thus, as a result of interacting with the public, historical expectations, and individual views of the office, the person "becomes" president.

4. The office of the presidency dictates the nature and relationship of the president with the public.

5. Rhetoric, broadly defined, is the means to confirm or deny the public's expectations of acceptable role behavior.

6. Since Franklin D. Roosevelt, each succeeding president has (and will continue to have) less of an impact upon the character of the institutional presidency.

7. A successful presidential campaign and presidency is primarily one of marketing or product positioning. This means that a successful president is one who "mirrors" or nurtures preexisting beliefs, attitudes, and values of the public.

While these generalizations are broad in scope and not particularly startling, they do reflect my primary research approach, biases, and concerns: the rhetorical dimensions of the American presidency.

Acknowledgments

Writing a book is like building a house. Although there may be one architect or builder, the end result is the product of many hands. I gratefully acknowledge the financial support and assistance of Northern Illinois University from James Norris, Dean of the College of Liberal Arts and Sciences, as well as Jerrold Zar, Dean of the Graduate School, for the awarding of a Grant from the Dean's Fund for Research in 1986 and 1987. The university library was most helpful in lending and locating necessary materials.

I am especially indebted to Lisa Goodnight, my research assistant, who spent countless hours tracking down material, copying hundreds of pages, and always showing enthusiasm for the ideas and content of this project. Her untiring efforts, unquestionable loyalty, and total belief in the book often served as a source of motivation and inspiration. I can only hope that she is as lucky in finding as capable an assistant in her future academic career. Thanks Lisa.

Colleagues are invaluable and contribute directly and indirectly to all scholarly endeavors. For the support and encouragement of departmental friends I am most appreciative.

Finally, thank goodness there is life beyond academe. In what appears to be a pattern, as I was attempting to give birth to this book, my wife gave birth to another son. Happily, Paula, Bobby, and Christopher provided an excuse to turn the manuscript in late. Their love and support are the true difference between success and failure.

1
Ronald Reagan as "The Great Communicator"

Ronald Reagan, "the Great Communicator," has enjoyed tremendous personal popularity despite obvious gaffes, poor grasp of issues, and even harmful policy decisions.[1] In 1984, he received more votes than any politician in the history of our country.[2] Reagan, a professed conservative, received majorities in virtually every voter block or group in the population. For the first time since the days of Lyndon Johnson, more Americans were satisfied than unsatisfied.

Analysts praise Reagan's ability to project an image of warmth and sincerity while also showing strength and resolve. Gerald Pomper and his colleagues summarize the 1984 presidential election as Americans voting for a likeable person who uses stirring rhetoric, a defender of religion and the family.[3] But Reagan's second term, full of promise, ends in embarrassment and unfulfilled promises. As Isaac Asimov notes, "I'm afraid that Ronald Reagan has, in a sense, weakened and trivialized the presidency, that he has, for a long time now, made it more important for a president to be popular than to be effective."[4]

As a student and scholar of presidential communication, I must confess that the label of "the Great Communicator" never came to mind in relation to Ronald Reagan. It is impossible to find a Reagan speech that compares to Jefferson's inaugural address that describes the values, goals, and purposes of government; or Lincoln's first inaugural address that promotes unity, or his second inaugural that promises forgiveness; or Franklin Roosevelt's inaugural address that brought comfort and hope to the Depression era audience; or Kennedy's inaugural address that stirred the minds and imaginations of the American people. It is impossible to find a Reagan speech that is as eloquent as Lincoln's address at Gettysburg; as informed as Wilson's address in support of the League of Nations; as confident as Franklin Roosevelt's declaration of war message; as impassioned as Kennedy's Berlin Wall address; or as committed as Johnson's declaration of war on poverty. It is simply impossible to find a Reagan speech that will be studied as a piece of literature or as an exemplary example of human persuasion.

Yet, without doubt, future Americans will be shown clips of Reagan asserting himself in an early 1980 presidential debate, congratulating U.S. Olympians, standing on the shores of Normandy and before troops in Korea, saluting the Tomb of the Unknown Soldier, comforting the widow of a slain American soldier, and presiding at the Statue of Liberty celebration. The fact is that America has always had great communicators. Our political and social leaders have been those who master the communications technology of their age.[5]

Andrew Jackson utilized a friendly newspaper, the *Washington Globe,* to espouse his policies. Theodore Roosevelt, a master of public relations, understood the impact of delivering powerful messages reprinted in daily newspapers with dramatic photographs. He seldom refused a photo opportunity. Woodrow Wilson, while lacking personal charisma, initiated regular press conferences and even commissioned motion pictures to capture newsworthy events. Franklin Roosevelt, of course, mastered the media of radio and motion pictures. And now we have Ronald Reagan being proclaimed as a "great communicator"—and he is great largely because of his mastery of the television medium.

THE CHANGING NATURE OF POLITICAL RHETORIC

As society and technology change, so do the ways presidents campaign and govern. As a result, presidential rhetoric has undergone a fundamental change in both form and content. Barnet Baskerville argues, in a book entitled *The People's Voice,* that "societal values and attitudes are reflected not only in what the speaker says but also in how he says it—not only in the ideas and arguments to be found in speeches of the past but in the methods and practices of representative speakers and in the role and status accorded speakers by the listening public. As public tastes and public needs change, so do speaking practices—types of appeal, verbal style, modes of delivery."[6]

The United States has a rich history of political oratory. For much of our history, public oratory provided the main avenue to success and popular esteem. Politicians were expected to frequently make long public orations. Such occasions were public spectacles with banners, bands, slogans, and fireworks. The famous "soap box" or "stump" campaigns were deliberative in nature. Politicians articulated elements of political philosophy. During the golden ages, political oratory was an instrument for conducting national business and a means of public education, and served as an end in itself—a mode of creative expression.

By 1900 political oratory had undergone its first fundamental change. This change was signaled by Lincoln in his Gettysburg Address. He established a trend toward brevity and simplicity in public oratory. But more important was the shift of the American hero from the politician to the businessman. Captains of industry espoused virtues of directness, conciseness, and pragmatism. Political speeches became shorter, more colloquial, and less "airy." In fact, political oratory became public speaking with an emphasis on utility of message and the sharing of information. The number of magazine articles and newspaper stories increased while their length decreased. Radio introduced lively discussion shows, news "reports" (unlike news stories), and time constraints upon both the speaker and audience.

Thus, there was a shift in the attitudes of Americans toward politicians, work and industry, and the outside world. The shift of attitudes also impacted how we talked to each other. Radio crossed ethnic and regional boundaries. Politicians had to speak "at" audiences, not "with" audiences. The press became "filters" rather than "vehicles" of political communication.

It was television, as you may have guessed, that initiated the third major change in political campaign rhetoric. The details of this change will be discussed later. An important argument of this book, however, is that after nearly 30 years of the television medium, we now have a mature and complete television president in the form of Ronald

Reagan. In the 1970s, campaign politics was viewed as a mature science. The professionals believed the key to success was "poli-techs" or the use of computers to track voters and assist in precinct canvasing and direct mail activities.[7] The better financed Republicans utilized such technology primarily because of scattered and rural party members. Democrats relied on organized labor and other groups to mobilize voters and garner support. Today, the key is "video politics." This does not refer to policy discussion or political commercials but to the control and manipulation of local and national nightly news presentations. Campaigning and governing are done through the medium of television. As early as 1974, Kevin Phillips proclaimed that "in the age of the mass media, the old Republican and Democratic parties have lost their logic. Effective communications are replacing party organizations as the key to political success. . . . As the first communications society, the United States is on its way to becoming the first 'mediacracy'."[8] We are witnessing the evolution of the "new presidential" rhetoric that differs in both form and content from that of only 20 years ago. It is useful to briefly focus on some of these changes.

Form Changes

The most obvious and important impact upon modern presidential campaigning is the shift from face-to-face to mediated communication. Electronic media, according to Roderick Hart's study, "simplify the message, invigorate it, but make it less uplifting and less personal than do local circumstances . . . Television gives us a one-dimensional presidency."[9] The media place their own requirements upon style of presentation, length of presentation, and content of messages.

Second, presidential rhetoric today is more ceremonial than deliberative. Presentations have become ritualized in form and content. Gone are the days of ideological discussion and free debate. Public presentations are designed to gain acknowledgment and acceptance, and serve as the ultimate pep rally.

Presidential addresses have become monologues rather than dialogues. The immediate audiences are largely ignored in favor of the evening news and tomorrow's headlines. Thus, the role and the function of the audience has changed in the modern presidential campaign. The audience becomes "viewers" with individual choice and control over who and what they allow into their living rooms.

Finally, in campaigns, political ads have become the primary form of campaign rhetoric. Kathleen Jamieson claims that "political advertising is now the major means by which candidates for the presidency communicate their messages to voters."[10] The ads provide name recognition, identify the issues, present the persona, and articulate the reasons for election. Yet, many of those ads do not have the candidate directly speaking, or if so, they serve only as "masters of ceremonies." As critics, we must treat political ads as public addresses. Jamieson concurs and argues that we should view campaign advertising "as an extended message rather than a series of discrete message units . . . Advertising is rarely anything but a digest of the speeches being delivered throughout the country."[11] The personal speaking appearances of candidates are not meant to become the means of mass persuasion but rather to reinforce the ads and to serve as a method of gaining additional television exposure. Political advertising has become the political oratory of this age.

Content Changes

The form changes of presidential campaign rhetoric also dictate the content changes. Ironically, as the speed of communication and information increases, the elements of democratic delegation and representation become less satisfying. Constituents become directly involved in the day-to-day affairs of state vicariously through the media. The stress of citizen involvement has moved from action to reaction, from initiator to responder. Political messages, then, no longer can take the time to justify and explain. Rather, they provide summaries and conclusions. Issues are identified but not debated. Solutions are offered freely with little or no reasons for the problems given. Campaign addresses are highly personalized with many self-references. While the style of presentation is more emotional, the content is less complex or ideological.

The primary concerns of presidential rhetoric are in projecting images rather than reasoning and icons of leadership rather than management. Clearly, how something is said is more important than what is said, and the act becomes primary to the message or actually becomes the message.

Reasons for the Changes in Presidential Rhetoric

I think there are three reasons or influences that have fundamentally altered presidential campaign rhetoric. The first, of course, is television. Its impact simply cannot be minimized. It makes every action public and by doing so trivializes both issues and candidates. It becomes impossible to distinguish the difference in importance between the shouting down of a rude audience member and the candidate's position on nuclear disarmament. Television, as a medium, is best suited for answers, not questions; solutions, not problems; and good old-fashioned "horse sense," not wisdom. These characterizations will be discussed in greater detail in Chapters 2 and 3.

The second major influence upon the nature of presidential rhetoric today is the fact that politics is big business. Political campaigns have become one-day sale events in which customers must come to the voting booth to confirm their purchase or preference of candidate. The professionalization of political communication has created an industry and a true "professional politician." The consulting industry dictates when, what, where, and how candidates communicate to the public. Communication techniques and strategies replace political issues and positions. Today's professional politicians are paid for managing and winning elections. For them, politics is a permanent, continual campaign and not the process of governing. And, as I will argue in Chapter 4, all incumbents must have their own professional staffs whose primary function is to stage and present the administration to the American public, primarily through the medium of television.

Finally, how we nominate presidential candidates, along with various rule changes in that process, impact the form and content of campaign rhetoric—not to mention the type of candidates we get to run for office. For example, the new rules for selection in the 1988 presidential campaign greatly affected the form and content of campaign rhetoric. There were fewer open primaries (only 17, compared to 30 in 1972), which meant greater appeal to party loyalty, and the new regional southern primary made the early leaders almost unbeatable. Although the presidential campaigns actually started earlier and advertising was "frontloaded," there was less time and need for early leaders in the race to discuss or develop issues. Money and organization are the most critical elements in the primary campaign.

THE PUBLIC PRESIDENCY

Today we have what many scholars refer to as "a public presidency."[12] Samuel Kernell makes the argument that presidents "going public" is a strategic adaptation to the information age. "Going public," Kernell calls "a leadership style consistent with the requirements of a political community that is increasingly susceptible to the centrifugal forces of public opinion."[13] Thus, he predicts that "going public" will occupy a prominent place in the strategic repertoire of future presidents.

Roderick Hart's rhetorical model of the presidency consists of four dimensions, all of which address the form and content of contemporary public presidential persuasion.[14] The strategic dimension assumes that anything a president says or does is noted and has impact; that the most important policy decision confronting a president is not elements of policy but how to articulate the policy; and that presidential actions give meaning to national rituals. The creative dimension focuses on how presidents articulate policy, define situations, and justify actions. The projective dimension identifies and specifies elements of presidential images of leadership and performance. The corporate dimension focuses on the presidential "persuasion factory" of professional wordsmiths and media consultants.

Hart's latest study reveals that presidents are talking to us more than ever before, primarily because of the mass media. He concludes that "presidential speechmaking—perhaps presidential communication in general—has now become a tool of barter rather than a means of informing and challenging the citizenry."[15]

Thus, why and how our presidents talk to us have changed a great deal over the last 200 years. These changes correspond not so much to international or geopolitics as to the evolution of our communication technologies. Television is now the dominant medium, which not only alters why and how presidents communicate but the kind of leader we recruit. Ronald Reagan has become the model for the primetime president. He succeeded where other contemporary presidents such as Johnson, Nixon, Ford, and Carter failed.

"THE GREAT COMMUNICATOR"

There are three broad explanations that account for Reagan's success as "the Great Communicator." First, there is a cultural explanation. Reagan has reestablished the "heroic presidency" and reinforced perceptions of U.S. myths and values. Myth bridges the old and the new. Myth is composed of images from the past that help us cope with and understand the present. Myth functions to reduce the complexity of the world by identifying causes that are simple and remedies that are apparent. He can be tough with foreign nations, Congress, criminals, and just bad, lazy people. He believes most Americans are good, moral, hardworking, and optimistic about the future. For him, the United States' heritage is one of freedom, faith, courage, commitment, determination, and generosity. With Reagan, Americans saw the president of an idealized past who defined the citizens in textbook terms of "patriotism, motherhood, and apple pie."

Second, Reagan carefully managed the symbolic vestments of the presidency. Reagan's public presentations were carefully planned and orchestrated. Image control was of prime importance to the Reagan staff.[16] Early in his administration, Reagan significantly increased the parties, dinners, and receptions at the White House. The old presidential yacht *Sequoia* was returned and new dinner china purchased. "Class" was restored to the White House—and the public loved it. It is an interesting paradox of the American presidency that we like the notion of a common man, one of us running for president. But once elected, we demand uncommon leadership, great insight, and vast knowledge from our presidents. A president must appear presidential as defined by history, culture, and status of the position. Carter was often criticized for his lack of presidential behavior, dress, and demeanor. Such incidents as Carter carrying his own luggage and wearing blue jeans at the White House became instant news stories.

Finally, Reagan's use of the media not only provides access to the general public but virtually guarantees favorable reception of Reagan and his "personality." It is this latter element that is the focus of the book. The thrust of my argument, however, is not so much on how television has changed politics in the U.S. or how Ronald Reagan manipulated media content, but how Ronald Reagan conforms to the essential needs and characteristics of television as a medium. Reagan conformed to the form and content demands of television to take his message to the people. His acting skills, cinematic language, and orchestrated settings resulted in the election and reelection of one of the most popular presidents in U.S. history. In the 1960s, television became the instrument of winning elections. Reagan made it the instrument of governing. The medium became the message.

Ronald Reagan is a great communicator on television. In the following chapters, I discuss the growing influence of television on the institutional presidency, and identify the unique characteristics and requirements of the medium and how Reagan programmed and ran the primetime presidency. As of this writing no one has labeled Reagan "the great administrator," "the great leader," "the great policy maker," or "the great political philosopher." Without much risk, I doubt anyone will. Thus, in the last chapter, implications of the primetime presidency are discussed.

NOTES

1. Paul Light and Celinda Lake report that throughout the 1984 presidential campaign 70 percent of the voters liked Reagan personally while over half of them disapproved of his policies (p. 92). For more information see "The Election: Candidates, Strategies, and Decisions" in *The Election of 1984*, Michael Nelson, ed. (Washington, DC: Congressional Quarterly Press, 1985).

2. Gerald Pomper et al., *The Election of 1984* (Chatham, NJ: Chatham House Publishers, 1985), p. 60.

3. Pomper et al., *Election of 1984*, p. 79.

4. "Jennings Koppel Report: Memo to the Future," ABC News, April 23, 1987, transcript page 12.

5. For an excellent historical discussion, see Martin Schram, *The Great American Video Game* (New York: William Morrow & Co., 1987), pp. 64-80.

6. Barnet Baskerville, *The People's Voice* (Lexington, KY: University of Kentucky Press, 1979), p. 4.

7. Schram, *Great American Video Game*, pp. 27-28.

8. Kevin Phillips, *Mediacracy* (New York: Doubleday, 1974), p. v.

9. Roderick Hart, *Verbal Style and the Presidency* (Orlando, FL: Academic Press, 1984), pp. 57 and 54.

10. Kathleen Jamieson, *Packaging the Presidency* (New York: Oxford University Press, 1984), p. 446.

11. Jamieson, *Packaging the Presidency,* p. 451.

12. For example see Robert E. Denton, Jr. and Dan Hahn, *Presidential Communication* (New York: Praeger, 1986); Michael Grossman and Martha Kumar, *Portraying the President* (Baltimore, MD: Johns Hopkins University Press, 1981); Roderick Hart, *Verbal Style and the Presidency* (Orlando, FL: Academic Press, 1984); Roderick Hart, *The Sound of Leadership* (Chicago: University of Chicago Press, 1987); Samuel Kernell, *Going Public* (Washington, DC: Congressional Quarterly Press, 1986); Theodore Lowi, *The Personal President* (Ithaca, NY: Cornell University Press, 1985); and Jefferey Tulis, *The Rhetorical Presidency* (Princeton, NJ: Princeton University Press, 1987).

13. Kernell, *Going Public,* p. 212.

14. Hart, *Verbal Style and the Presidency,* pp. 6-8.

15. Hart, *The Sound of Leadership,* p. 212.

16. For numerous examples see Robert E. Denton, Jr. and Gary Woodward, *Political Communication in America* (New York: Praeger, 1985), especially Chapters 2, 3, and 7 and Robert E. Denton, Jr. and Dan Hahn, *Presidential Communication* (New York: Praeger, 1986), especially Chapters 2 and 7.

2
Mass Media and
the U.S. Presidency

In many ways the mass media have become the central nervous system of our society. Traditionally, scholars have recognized four basic functions of the mass media: information dissemination, persuasion (both commercial and political), entertainment, and cultural transmission.[1] Mass communication has several distinct characteristics.[2] In our country, the mass media are commercial. They are economic, capitalistic industries that are essential parts of our total economy. The audience of the mass media is large, anonymous, and most often heterogeneous. The messages are transient, rapidly transmitted, and provide little or no opportunity for immediate feedback. And the sources of the messages of mass communication are impersonal institutions that hire highly trained specialists to write and produce the messages we consume.

These characteristics highlight the differences among mass communication and other forms of communication. In addition to much larger audiences and reduced opportunities for feedback, there is greater competition for receiver attention because of channel noise (i.e., situational and contextual) and message repetition. Speed and accuracy of message transmission are not only major differences between mass communication and other forms but also are advantages of mass communication.

THE SOCIAL POWER OF THE MASS MEDIA

Scholars and lay people alike have historically recognized the social power of mass media.[3] The influence and role of the mass media in the electoral and governing processes have greatly increased. The various media have become the major source of information about politics. Americans receive political information from the media in three important ways: through political advertising, news stories, and feature stories. Such sources of information are perceived as more truthful and accurate than family or friends.

Harold Innis argues that control over communication media is a means through which social and political power is wielded.[4] For him, new media can break old political monopolies. He also observes that various media differ in their potentialities for control. A medium that requires special skill or limited access will most likely be exploited by an elite class. In contrast, an easily accessible medium tends to be more common and democratic. The media can quickly and efficiently attract, focus, and direct attention to social problems. In addition, the media can serve as channels for public persuasion and mobilization. In mobilizing groups or "kinds of public," the media also help sustain them and their causes. In doing so, the media confer status and legitimacy to groups, issues, or ideas. Increasingly, the media are recognized for providing psychic rewards and gratifications. While these powers are rather positive and beneficial, there are some less attractive powers and influences. In the 1960s, Marshall McLuhan observed that "the public, in the sense of a great consensus of separate and distinct viewpoints, is finished. Today, the mass audience (the successor to the 'public') can be used as a creative participating force. It is, instead, merely given packages of passive entertainment."[5] The media have an impact upon feelings and emotions as well as influencing the beliefs, attitudes, and values of individuals. As a result, the media can influence individual and group behavior.

Joshua Meyrowitz, in a most interesting analysis, argues that the impact of the media upon social behavior is "not through the power of their messages but by reorganizing the social settings in which people interact and by weakening the once-strong relationship between physical place and social 'place'."[6] Physical presence is no longer a prerequisite for first-hand experience of the world. The evolution of the media has decreased the significance of physical presence and has altered the significance of time and space for social interaction. Distances, oceans, mountains, and walls no longer isolate and separate people from the "outside world." Information, however defined, is a commodity and accessible to various social groups. Thus, what people see, experience, and learn have nothing to do with age, sex, income, or education.

David Altheide and Robert Snow posit that the media collectively are a form of communication that has a logic of its own. Media logic is the interactive process through which media present and transmit information.[7] Elements of the logic include organization, style of presentation, focus on elements of behavior, and the grammar of the media used. These elements impact social institutions such as politics, religion, or sports to create a unique "media culture." The major point is that when media is used to present the form or content of an institution, the very form and content of the institution is altered. A key part of this process is the audience's perception and interpretation of a particular medium's messages. As a technology, the modern media carry a connotation of rationality. Because of this, according to Altheide and Snow, both communicator and audience are oriented toward a "rational means-end" type of communication. Audiences view the information shared to be accurate, objective, and current. As a society, we have become dependent upon the media. Pictures and visions make the world understandable and shape the environment. What is projected affects what is seen. People, of course, see things differently.

The obvious danger is when the media become the means through which events and ideas are interpreted and acted upon. The media often create "experts" who become credible, knowledgeable, etc., and "personalities" whose real fame rests with the media. The media can take people of limited notoriety and make them "authorities," offering advice on a whole range of topics regardless of their credentials. For example, why should Alan Alda be viewed as an expert on sex relations or Robert Redford on ecology? The media, because of its logic or function, legitimizes "reality" by determining the subjects to be discussed, creating "experts" on various subjects, being the source and constructor of information, history, etc., and reinforcing their own practices to create further dependence. Today, social institutions use the media to define and solve problems, such as the "Just Say No" drug campaign of 1987.

Thus, mediated communication is a unique form of communication. It differs significantly from other forms of communication. In addition, mass communication has become an integral and essential form in our society. Its role and influence in the political process are equally important.

MASS MEDIA AND POLITICS

William Spragens identifies four periods of growth and development of media's impact upon our political system.[8] The first period, 1789 to 1860, was a time of newspaper dominance and party-oriented press. Newspapers presented detailed discussions and viewpoints about issues. The newspapers served as the forums for political debates. By the 1830s, political parties sponsored their own newspapers dedicated to propagandizing the party's issue positions.

The second period, 1860 to 1900, experienced the development of new media technologies. The rise of the wire services helped to nationalize news and standardize coverage of events. As the U.S. became primarily a two-party system, metropolitan newspapers such as the *New York Times* became a major force in politics. The editors of such newspapers became well-known public figures and influential within party politics.

In the next period, 1900 to 1950, syndicated columnists, whose work was published nationwide, displaced editors in having more influence upon national politics. Of course, the introduction of radio changed forever the nature of U.S. politics primarily because of the immediacy and intimacy of the medium. The public could hear the actual candidates and politicians respond to various situations and events. Soon, however, radio commentators grew in popularity and importance as had the syndicated newspaper columnists.

The final period for Spragens is 1950 to the present. A new medium, television, once again changed the nature and practice of politics forever. By the mid-1960s, television viewership exceeded readership of newspapers. Television networks began to interpret events and provide investigative reporting. Television made the world smaller, more immediate, and even more relevant. In many ways, television provided a single audience but countless constituencies. The complexity of campaigning and governing increased while the requirements of presentation simplified.

I would argue with Professor Spragens that a fifth period of media impact began in 1980. In the aftermath of Watergate and the Vietnam War, the media took the initiative in confronting politicians and defining social reality. Television matured as a technology and became *the* instrument that links the public to government and to the general society. The important linkage role of the media is performed in three ways: by providing information to the public, providing interpretation, and functioning as a conduit for messages that possess unique medium-specific characteristics. This book explores, from a television perspective, those dimensions.

Within the academic community, there has always been a great debate about the specific effects of media upon our political process. Since the 1940s, studies have generally argued that the main impact of media is to activate predispositions and reinforce attitudes rather than to convert voters. Christopher Arterton, however, questions the "minimal effects" assumptions of the research.[9] For him, many of the studies viewed exposure to media as the cause for attitude variation rather than as an element of possible impact. It is difficult to find subjects who are not exposed to any television and to define "heavy users" versus "light users" of television in relation to impact, retention, and importance. Also, most of the research was conducted only during elections when, indeed, most opinions are set. It is the time between elections that is most critical in voter attitude, image, and issue formation.[10] Many of the studies simply ignore the phases of campaigns when importance and impact of media may differ. Finally, few studies recognize the importance of the "agenda-setting" function of the media.

According to William Adams, there are four broad perspectives on media effects.[11] The "impotence" perspective views media influence as much less than that of family, friends, and socioeconomic variables. The "virility" perspective views the media as very powerful and persuasive. Media's selection of stories and methods of coverage literally create social reality to which we respond. The last two perspectives focus on specific media as welders of great power and influence. "Print power" perspective argues that newspapers have the most direct impact upon citizen attitudes of any media. In contrast, "video power" argues that television is the king maker and king breaker, especially in presidential politics.

I think it is important to note that regardless of the research findings, the absence of medium effects does not mean the absence of media effects. I also agree that today, as never before, television is a powerful medium that impacts campaigning and the governing of our nation. The next chapter focuses on the latter issue in greater detail.

Perhaps the term "media effects" connotes too strong a deterministic notion and "media influence" is more palatable. Robert Denton and Gary Woodward argue that

the mass media influence American politics in three princi-
pal ways.[12] First, in relation to the above criticism, the
mass media collectively exert a considerable influence on
determining the agenda of topics for public discussion,
debate, and action. Not only is there a limit to the number
of issues, topics, etc. that should or can receive public attention, but the selection of specific concerns increasingly
lies with the mass communication industries rather than
with citizens or public officials. It is difficult for politicians
to initiate, establish, or maintain social agendas without
the help and participation of the mass media industries.
Politicians most often find themselves in the role of responder rather than initiator of public issues.

It should also be noted that the public "allows" for the
media influence because of the dependence it has upon the
media. We expect the media to investigate issues, ask candidates questions for us, and keep public officials honest. If
asked, I doubt many Americans would favor a mere
"reporting" of information without synthesis, selection,
and interpretation. In addition, public officials and politicians use the media to convey ideas, share information, and
attempt to solve social problems. As a result, we should
recognize the interdependent relationship we have with
the media.

Certainly related to the above notion, the media give
form and substance to world events. They construct our
political realities, telling us who is good or bad, right or
wrong, strong or weak, just or unjust. Media "snapshots"
of the world become the "album" of both our knowledge
and memories of the outside world. In addition to telling us
what to think about, the media also tell us how to think.
With the reporting of the facts comes a subsequent judg-
ment. There is always a conclusion, point, or reason for a

presentation, but there is little or no time for synthesis or analysis. Awareness is valued more than understanding. It is also rather ironic, despite the perception of an adversarial relationship with government officials, that these officials benefit more from mass media presentations than do outsiders or critics of elected officials. In a study by Leon Sigal, government officials provided 75 percent of all news stories, and less than one percent of all news stories were based on reporters' own analyses.[13] In addition, 90 percent of the stories were based on messages of key actors in the stories. Seldom do politicians speak for themselves. Reporters act as narrators and interpreters, assessing the motives or consequences of political actions or events. And political realities are constructed to conform to the demands of the medium, demands that seem best satisfied by melodrama. Melodramatic images of foolishness, villainy, and heroism are common. The themes used to outline many stories are constant: the triumph of the individual over adversity, justice winning over evil, redemption of the individual through reform, and the rewarding of valor or heroism.

Finally, the media reduce abstract or ideological principles to human, personal components. Political issues and actions are linked to individuals. We have choices not among policies but among actors. Victims, villains, and heroes are easier to identify and address than issues, causes, or ideas. Television is especially a "personalistic" medium. With television the presenter dominates. It is a medium for actors and animate objects. To some extent, the personalizing nature of the mass media has contributed to the decline and lack of interest in party organizations and smaller political jurisdictions.

In essence, the mass media have changed politics in two significant ways.[14] First, the nature of political participation has changed. As McLuhan early observed, "a new form of 'politics' is emerging and in ways we haven't yet noticed. The living room has become a voting booth."[15] Second, the content of politics has changed. Few citizens learn about politics through direct experience. Our political knowledge, as already noted, is mediated. And the mediated process, according to Dan Nimmo and James Combs, results "as much in the creation, transmission, and adoption of political fantasies as realistic views of what takes place."[16] Again, McLuhan addressed this point years ago. He argued that television was too "cool" to handle properly hot issues and sharply defined controversial topics. "As a cool medium TV has, some feel, introduced a kind of rigor mortis into the body politic. It is the extraordinary degree of audience participation in the TV medium that explains its failure to tackle hot issues."[17] Thus, politics becomes an activity of style over substance, image over reality, melodrama over analysis, belief over knowing, awareness over understanding.

MASS MEDIA AND THE PRESIDENCY

Presidents are responsible to the public and thus must maintain good relations. Relations with the public are important to presidents because they directly affect his political survival, ability to perform his job well, and establishment of a positive historical image.[18] According to Doris Graber, the quality of interaction between presidents and the public depends on three things.[19] The first factor is the quality and quantity of communication channels. The channels need to be adequate in number and comprehensive and open to allow sufficient access. The second factor in assessing the quality of interaction between presidents and the public is the communication skills of the president. Such skills include the ability to use television, dramatize issues, and persuade the public when support for an issue is needed. The final factor affecting presidential and public interaction is the general political climate of the interaction. The president's primary access to the public is through the mass media.

It is through the mass media that we come to know our presidents. And with the frequency of appearance we have come to know our presidents intimately. Any piece of information about the president, no matter how trivial or private, is newsworthy, ranging from Carter's hemorrhoids to Reagan's much more serious colon cancer surgery.

Roderick Hart and several colleagues have identified six perspectives from which various groups of citizens view the presidential relationship with the mass media.[20] The "no bias" perspective maintains that the media merely pass along what the president says with no interpretation or bias. Despite contentions to the contrary from those in the news business, few scholars or even the general public believe this perspective.

The "liberal bias" perspective, vigorously argued by Vice President Spiro Agnew in 1972, is still prominent today. The argument contends that the media are controlled by liberals who are far from objective in their presentations. In fact, some argue that the media only address liberal concerns, issues, candidates, or policies. Thus, those who accept this perspective believe conservative positions not only receive little serious attention, but in fact receive negative treatment in the media. Today there are several networks whose primary purpose is to counter the perceived liberal bias, such as CBN, USA, or the PTL networks, to name only a few.

Ironically, however, an effective argument can be made that there is a "conservative bias" in the primary relationship between the president and the press. The basis for the belief in a conservative bias of the media lies in media support of corporate capitalism and other status quo positions. By extension, then, the media support presidential efforts of fiscal conservatism and, through their support of the status quo, are essentially anti-liberal in their orientation.

The fourth orientation, "presidential bias," holds that the media are really captive to the presidential office. Presidents have almost immediate and unlimited access to the media and thus the national audience. And when considering the efforts of the White House staff to control media events and image, it is nearly impossible to truly counter the powerful stronghold the president has over the media.

The "organizational bias" perspective provides a more sociological explanation of presidential-press relations. The emphasis of this perspective is on the power of the mass media organizations, a power that supposedly is great enough to allow the media to dictate what is covered and how material is presented. Even the geographic location of news organizations in New York and Washington is said to greatly influence the treatment and selection of stories.

The final perspective, the "rhetorical bias," posits that all mediated messages are formulated based upon recognized rules. These accepted "rules" conform to media requirements of presentation and dictate the style, form, and even content of news presentations.

There appear to be three phases in presidential-press relations.[21] First is the alliance phase, in which cooperation is the rule; for the president it is a "honeymoon" period.

As a result, presidents receive good and favorable coverage. Early in a new administration, the press is dependent upon the White House staff to provide information and presidential access. The competitive phase begins when reporters start looking for conflicts within an administration, especially among Cabinet officials. The White House becomes irritated and attempts to counter reporters by presenting their side of the stories. The president remains visible but must now confront more hostile questions and speculations. The final phase is one of detachment. As the White House staff becomes more frustrated, they limit the access of the national media. The president adopts a "rose garden" strategy. Local and smaller presses receive good treatment. Because of the cautious and distrustful attitude of the president, surrogates are used to articulate the administration's views.

In addition to the phases of presidential-press relations, Frank Kessler identifies specific attitudes or perspectives presidents tend to have toward the press.[22] Some presidents are rather indifferent or aloof in terms of the press. Dwight Eisenhower received great public support. As a war hero, he was very self-confident and felt little need to appease the press.

Some presidents, according to Kessler, develop a respectful-manipulative attitude for the press. Here presidents understand the adversarial relationship with the press and attempt to provide maximum access to ensure favorable coverage. Franklin Roosevelt, Harry Truman, and John Kennedy are examples of this perspective. Roosevelt held frequent and intimate press conferences. Although somewhat skeptical, Truman held weekly press conferences. Kennedy was perhaps the first to make a science of manipulating news coverage. He nurtured those who

gave him and his administration favorable coverage.
Rewards included personal interviews, briefings, and
visits.

On the other extreme, some presidents come to office
with a suspicious-vindictive perspective. Lyndon Johnson
thought the "Eastern Harvard boys" were out to get him.
He blamed the press for his domestic problems and the lack
of support for his Vietnam policy. For Johnson, you were
either with him or against him. Richard Nixon, however,
actually sought to "get even" with hostile press members.
In a memo to Stuart Magruder, Nixon suggested that the
Federal Communications Commission (FCC) monitor
network news programs, the Justice Department review
media for violations of law, and the Internal Revenue
Service (IRS) be encouraged to examine media finances.
Without doubt, Nixon was the most vindictive of all U.S.
presidents toward the press.

Finally, Kessler argues that Gerald Ford and Jimmy
Carter are examples of presidents who had a respectful-
deferential attitude toward the press. This approach is
usually adopted by presidents who have no national relationship with the press and must attempt to gain one. It
was important for Ford to get a media person to act as
press secretary. Jody Powell was directed by Carter to be
honest and forthright with the press. Neither Carter nor
Ford had the personal charisma to command media attention that Roosevelt, Kennedy, or Reagan had.

Regardless of the nature of the relationship between the
press and the president, they each desperately need the
other. In the 1960s, televised coverage of the presidency
and political campaigns became a primary occupation of
the news media. Since that time "image," "audience
share," "targeting," "packaging," "teleprompter," and a

host of other terms have become a part of the political lexicon. Presidents and potential presidents, since Theodore Roosevelt turned the White House into the "bully pulpit," need to link their public persuasive efforts with the media. But today, the media equally need presidential "bits" of exposure and information to satisfy the public's curiosity and preoccupation with our chief executive. And the White House provides many services for the press. It provides background briefings, off-the-record comments, transcripts, and daily handouts, as well as granting access and interviews.

Rodger Streitmatter discovered in a recent study that presidential personality greatly impacts news coverage in major newspapers.[23] He found that a president whose personality appeals to the press receives 50 percent more coverage. After reviewing a sixty year period, Streitmatter concluded that robust, outgoing presidents received 49 percent more general news coverage and 87 percent more personal news coverage than quiet, more reserved presidents.

The result of this symbiotic relationship is a constant battle of presidential access and control. To use a medium effectively implies control, planning, and proper execution. For presidents, each category is a challenge, struggle, and process of adaptation. Perhaps the greatest challenge is to control news coverage to ensure that it is favorable to the incumbent. The presidents' press secretaries are the immediate links with the press. Although their function is to serve as a conduit of information, they must attempt to control the agenda as well as what is said and not said. There are, of course, several ways a president can attempt to control, or at least coordinate, news coverage. News or information favorable to the president is released from the

White House, whereas less favorable news is left unstated or released from other departments. All interviews and statements are channeled through one source, thus ensuring control and consistency over content. Timing and managing releases are also important techniques of news control. News items are often released in time to receive coverage on the evening news but not early enough to allow much time for full development or rebuttal. In addition, the release of two major stories in the same day is avoided. In a more active sense, presidents are always attempting to set the nation's agenda and goal priorities, creating "pseudo-events," and taking every opportunity to "plug" administration accomplishments, thus infusing the news with self-serving commercials.

Presidential press conferences, an obvious way for presidents to address the public, have become more and more problematic for officeholders to manage. Consequently, each president tends to have fewer and fewer. Franklin Roosevelt held about seven a month. Ronald Reagan held only seven in his first year as president.[24] Today, press conferences are much more public and formal. There is little true interaction and every president is aware that answers often receive replay several times, sometimes for several days. Modern presidents have tried a wide variety of tactics in order to reduce the risk associated with televised press conferences. Presidents Johnson and Nixon attempted to plant favorable questions among the reporters to ensure opportunities for presenting their views. In addition, Nixon used a blue curtain as a backdrop and got rid of the lectern to give a more calm, candid, and informal look to the press conferences. In April of 1984, Reagan changed the location of his televised press conferences. He now stands in the East Room of the White

House, before an open doorway that reveals a long, elegant corridor. The cameras record a majestic setting and a stately exit that dramatizes the importance of the office. Additionally, President Reagan requires the press members to raise their hands to be recognized, symbolically converting the reporters into school children.

To further ensure their success in the age of media politics, presidents and candidates have to rely upon the help and advice of consultants. They have become the new power in American politics. By 1950, advertising agencies handled most presidential electoral campaigns. But by 1970, most campaigns were directed by independent, individual political media specialists who coordinated the activities of media, advertising, public relations, and publicity. These consultants understand both the new technologies and the unique requirements of campaigning.

There are several reasons why officeholders and candidates need the service of consultants. First, the modern campaign is a complex endeavor, requiring highly specialized tasks such as advertising, research, and fundraising. It is unrealistic to expect candidates to have the technical expertise or the time to manage these activities in addition to campaigning or governing. The electoral process itself also places unique requirements upon candidates and campaigns. Direct voter contact is simply not possible and media coverage is, as already noted, the only exposure the average citizen has to the candidates. Consequently, the special requirements of the mass media have increased the need for consultants. To use a medium requires knowledge of the medium—its strengths, weaknesses, and nature. The growth of political consultants is directly related to the growth of the mass media and communication technologies. And finally, consultants are needed today because of what Sidney Blumenthal calls "the permanent campaign."[25] Governing the nation has become a perpetual campaign in which public support is constantly being sought.

Presidents have even had to adapt their language and speaking style to the requirements of the media, making sure they provide the ten-second answer designed to fit the demands of a news story. As Roderick Hart observes, "radio and television have changed how our presidents talk. The president in our living rooms bears only partial resemblance to the president speaking in the courthouse square."[26] Presidential discourse has become less personal, more simple, and less passionate. The personal stamp is gone and the human touch is media-created.

Media have changed the way presidents govern and must govern. They dictate the form and consequently the content of issues and policies. The mass media become the primary link to the public. Donna Cross posits that many of our earlier presidents probably would not have succeeded in today's media world.[27] Consider Washington's wig and false teeth, Lincoln's unpleasant looks and high pitched voice, Grant's alcoholism, or Franklin Roosevelt's wheelchair. Even in presidential newscasts, conflict and drama are the key elements of presentation and the commentators are the stars.[28] At best, according to Hart, the media gives us a one-dimensional presidency. "It presents our presidents to us in their Sunday best but without their souls or feelings."[29]

MASS MEDIA AND PRESIDENTIAL CAMPAIGNS

Much has been written about political campaigns, and few would argue with Thomas Patterson's assessment that "today's presidential campaign is essentially a mass media campaign."[30] As already hinted, I take issue with the basic assumption that political campaigns do not play a significant role in election results. Too much research has focused on voter conversion. Such research tends to ignore the long-term, subtle, and cumulative effects of politics and campaigns. Campaigns, in a broad sense, are complex exercises in the creation, re-creation, and transmission of significant symbols through communication. Communication activities are the vehicles for action.

Samuel Becker characterizes our communication environment as a "mosaic."[31] The mosaic consists of an infinite number of information "bits" or fragments on an infinite number of topics scattered over time and space. In addition, the bits are disorganized, and exposure is varied and repetitive. As these bits are relevant or address a need, they are attended. Thus, as we attempt to make sense of our environment, our current state of existence, political bits are elements of our voting choice, world view, or legislative desires. As voters, we must arrange these bits into a cognitive pattern that comprises our mosaic of a candidate, issue, or situation. Campaigns, then, are great sources of potential information and contain, however difficult to identify or measure, elements that impact upon decision making. Information bits can replace other bits to change or modify our world view, attitudes, or opinions.

It is important, however, to recognize the differences between news and politics. The mass media are first of all businesses. They require audiences in order to make money and turn a profit. Ratings are of great concern to news personalities, and news programming is very expensive. At best, news organizations are secondarily concerned about political values or issue dissemination. Thus, politicians and journalists have separate and distinct motives. Second, as already noted, the media dominate the creation of political agendas—not the politicians. For example, in the 1984 presidential campaign, the Geraldine Ferraro tax case dominated all newscasts and newspaper coverage for days. "No policy issue during the entire campaign," according to Thomas Patterson and Richard Davis, "commanded this level of news attention. Indeed, policy issues usually were not mentioned in the headlines or covered for more than a day or two consecutively."[32] Finally, the media have unique requirements that dictate how issues and candidates are treated. Television prefers, in order to hold viewer attention, personalized drama, action, conflict, and immediacy. A "horse race" is more appealing than a landslide; an individual is more appealing than an issue; the deviant or novel is better than the everyday or normal.

But just as the press and presidents need each other in nonelection years, they need each other even more so during campaigns. For journalists, elections are great news events; for campaigners they provide a way to reach the voters and obtain office. The importance of the media in campaigns has especially increased since political parties have declined in influence, the number of primaries have increased, and the campaign finance law of 1974 has restricted individual financial gifts.

So what are the effects of today's media campaigns and presidential elections? At the very least the role of the mass media has caused quantitative and qualitative changes in presidential elections.[33] From a quantitative perspective, there are simply more campaign messages than ever before in the form of news coverage, debates, political advertising, and pseudo-events. Qualitative changes are equally as noticeable. Campaigns have become more sophisticated and "slick," utilizing media techniques of presentation. Political strategy consists of market groups rather than geographic groups. And the entire campaign process has become depersonalized.

Richard Rubin uses the term "electoral circuitry" to describe the relationship between mass communications and electoral institutions.[34] The press conducts the flow of communication downward from political elites to the citizens and upward from the public to the elite. Thus, for him, "the very structures of key electoral institutions both respond to and are transformed by the intensity and velocity of mass communication."[35] Politicians believe the media are critical and thus act accordingly. By acting, they are changing the framework of political competition, expectations, campaigning, and governing.

While folk wisdom holds that one effect of the media has been that candidates' messages have changed from issue and policy concerns to those of image and personality, that is a misleading oversimplification. After all, the candidates still talk about issues and policy, so, in a sense, the content is the same. But there are media-created differences. For one, if you place a contemporary campaign speech beside one of 50 years ago, you find that the contemporary speech is much shorter, probably only about one-third as long, and it is comprised of much shorter paragraphs. The longer paragraphs of yesteryear contained arguments, which attempted to convert the audience; contemporary short paragraphs contain assertions and conclusions, which attempt to give the audience a position to identify with while simultaneously providing a 10- to 20-second pithy "bit" for the evening news. Additionally, some contemporary campaign speeches are given purely to establish image. When a liberal gives an anti-war speech to the American Legion convention or a conservative attacks welfare programs at a meeting of the NAACP, neither expects to convert the audience. Rather, the speeches are given for image reasons, to prove the speakers' courage, to prove that they can stand up to those opposed to their positions, and to prove they are not "wishy washy." Thus, while the messages of modern campaigners have not changed from issues to images, the structures of the messages and the motivations for them have. Electioneering politicians no longer try to convert through argumentation; rather, they attempt to say something we in the audience can identify with, to project an image by what they say, and to communicate something about their personalities by the audiences they choose to address.

Other specific media impacts also can be identified. The early stages of the nominating process are so unstructured that the press and media presentations can have great flexibility in structuring and defining political contests and issues. Thus, the media's greatest opportunity to influence the outcome of an election or campaign is in the primary period.[36] However, David Weaver and his colleagues report that in this early period only those truly interested in politics or the election pay any attention to media coverage.[37] Therefore, the media's greatest opportunity to influence the outcome of an election or campaign is when the majority of the audience is paying the least attention. In addition, Thomas Patterson and Robert McClure even question television's ability to transmit candidate images to the general public.[38] They also argue that political ads contain much more issue content than network newscasts. Weaver and his colleagues concur and assert that "despite large amounts of available information, most people learn very few dimensions of the candidate's image and even fewer aspects of issues."[39] Most political learning is that of awareness about issues without recall of relevant facts. Most news stories go unnoticed or are simply forgotten.

In reality, it is difficult to identify an area of presidential campaigns that is not impacted by the media. The media have influenced the role (or lack of role) of political parties, increased primaries, and even affected the campaign finance law. More generally, media impacts campaign issues, themes, and strategies. Key issues are those addressed by the media and reflect the interests of journalists. Campaigns are organized news events designed to gain coverage. Candidates who understand the media in all aspects will run the more successful campaigns. The true audience of a campaign is not the general public but the media barons.

Thus, rather than talking about media manipulation, it is better to describe media influence as that of "orchestration." To assert that the news media have no influence or impact is naive. But to assert that the news media "make or break" a campaign is equally misleading. I do think, however, that political campaigns have adjusted to the technical demands of the mass media. Presidential campaigns have changed drastically since 1952.

CONCLUSION

We began this chapter recognizing the fundamental impact of the mass media upon our society. The mass media not only changed the form, practice, and content of politics in the United States, but has also come to dictate the type of president we will have in the future. The marriage of politics and media started as one of convenience. It is difficult, at this point, to see who benefitted most from the arrangement. Few desire a divorce of the two. Perhaps the most we can ask for is mutual respect and understanding.

NOTES

1. These functions were first recognized by Harold Lasswell, "The Structure and Function of Communication in Society," *The Communication of Ideas,* Lyman Bryson, ed. (New York: Institute of Religious and Social Studies, 1948).

2. Kathleen Jamieson and Karlyn Campbell, *The Interplay of Influence* (Belmont, CA: Wadsworth, 1983), pp. 3-8.

3. See Dennis McQuail, "The Influence and Effects of Mass Media" in *Media Power in Politics,* Doris Graber, ed. (Washington, DC: Congressional Quarterly Inc., 1984), p. 50.

4. See Harold Innis, *The Bias of Communication,* rev. ed. (Toronto, Canada: University of Toronto Press, 1964) and *Empire and Communication,* rev. ed. (Toronto, Canada: University of Toronto Press, 1972).

5. Marshall McLuhan and Quentin Fiore. *The Medium Is the Message* (New York: Bantam Books, 1967), p. 22.

6. Joshua Meyrowitz, *No Sense of Place* (New York: Oxford University Press, 1985), p. ix.

7. David Altheide and Robert Snow, *Media Logic* (Beverly Hills, CA: Sage, 1979), pp. 9-10.

8. William Spragens, *The Presidency and the Mass Media in the Age of Television* (Lanham, MD: University Press of America, 1979), pp. 40-44.

9. Christopher Arterton, *Media Politics* (Lexington, MA: Lexington Books, 1984), pp. 5-6.

10. See Gary Mauser, *Political Marketing* (New York: Praeger, 1983).

11. William Adams, "Media Power in Presidential Elections" in *The President and the Public,* Doris Graber, ed. (Philadelphia, PA: Institute for Study of Human Issues, 1982), pp. 112-113.

12. Robert E. Denton, Jr. and Gary Woodward, *Political Communication in America* (New York: Praeger, 1984). See Chapter 6, especially pp. 146-162.

13. As reported in Lance Bennett, *News: The Politics of Illusion* (New York: Longman, 1983), pp. 53-54.

14. This argument was made in Robert E. Denton, Jr. and Dan Hahn's *Presidential Communication* (New York: Praeger, 1986). See p. 273.

15. Marshall McLuhan, *Understanding Media* (New York: New American Library, 1964), p. 22.

16. Dan Nimmo and James Combs, *Mediated Political Realities* (New York: Longman, 1983), p. xv.

17. McLuhan, *Understanding Media,* p. 269.

18. Doris Graber, "Introduction: Perspectives on Presidential Linkage" in *The President and the Public,* Doris Graber, ed. (Philadelphia, PA: Institute for Study of Human Issues, 1982), p. 2.

19. Graber, "Introduction," p. 7.

20. Roderick Hart, Patrick Jerome, and Karen McComb, "Rhetorical Features of Newscasts About the President," *Critical Studies in Mass Communication,* vol. 1, no. 3, September 1984, pp. 261-284.

21. Michael Grossman and Martha Kumar, *Portraying the President* (Baltimore, MD: Johns Hopkins University Press, 1981), pp. 273-298.

22. Frank Kessler, *The Dilemmas of Presidential Leadership* (Englewood Cliffs, NJ: Prentice-Hall, 1982), pp. 283-290.

23. Rodger Streitmatter, "The Impact of Presidential Personality on News Coverage in Major Newspapers," *Journalism Quarterly,* Spring 1985, pp. 66-73.

24. As reported in George Edwards, *The Public Presidency* (New York: St. Martin's Press, 1983), p. 112.

25. See Sidney Blumenthal, *The Permanent Campaign* (New York: A Touchstone Book, 1982).

26. Roderick Hart, *Verbal Style and the Presidency* (Orlando, FL: Academic Press, 1984), p. 54.

27. Donna Cross, *Media-Speak* (New York: Mentor Books, 1983), p. 205.

28. Hart et al., "Rhetorical Features of Newscasts About the President," pp. 261-284.

29. Hart, *Verbal Style and the Presidency*, p. 54.

30. Thomas Patterson, *The Mass Media Election* (New York: Praeger, 1980), p. 3.

31. Samuel Becker, "Rhetorical Studies for the Contemporary World," in *The Prospect for Rhetoric*, ed. Lloyd Bitzer and Edwin Black (Englewood Cliffs, NJ: Prentice-Hall, 1971), pp. 21-43.

32. Thomas Patterson and Richard Davis, "The Media Campaign: Struggle for the Agenda" in *The Election of 1984*, Michael Nelson, ed. (Washington, DC: Congressional Quarterly Press, 1985), p. 119.

33. The broad changes are discussed by Richard Joslyn, *Mass Media and Elections* (Reading, MA: Addison-Wesley, 1984).

34. Richard Rubin, *Press, Party, and Presidency* (New York: W.W. Norton, 1981), p. 4.

35. Rubin, *Press, Party, and Presidency*, p. 4.

36. See Donald Mathews, "The News Media and the 1976 Presidential Nominations" in *Race for the Presidency* (Englewood Cliffs, NJ: Prentice-Hall, 1978), pp. 56-57 and David Weaver, Doris Graber, Maxwell McCombs, and Chaim Eyal, *Media Agenda-Setting in Presidential Elections* (New York: Praeger, 1981), p. 74.

37. Weaver et al., *Media Agenda-Setting*, p. 26.

38. Thomas Patterson and Robert McClure, *The Unseeing Eye* (New York: Paragon Books, 1976), pp. 22-23.

39. Weaver et al., *Media Agenda-Setting*, p. 42.

3

Television and Presidential Politics

Aristotle argued that the size of an ideal society should be limited in order to protect the proper interactions among the governors and the governed. Aristotle concluded that "both in order to give decisions in matters of disputed rights, and to distribute the offices of government according to the merit of candidates, the citizens of a state must know one another's characters. Where this is not the case, the distribution of offices and the giving of decisions suffer."[1] Today, of course, it is only through the media that we can come to know our leaders. After the 1952 presidential election, RCA proclaimed in full-page newspaper ads, "television has brought their government back to the people!"[2] It is virtually impossible to distinguish between our political system and the media as separate entities. The result of our new form of politics is, as Marshall McLuhan and Quentin Fiore recognized, that "the living room has become the voting booth."[3]

Television has done more than simply reunite us with our leaders. Ironically, as the speed of communication and information increases, political delegation and representation become less satisfying. Constituents become directly involved in the day-to-day affairs of state by watching television news. The stress of citizen involvement has moved from action to reaction, from initiator to responder. Political messages no longer take the time to justify and explain. Rather, they provide summaries and conclusions. Television, as a medium, has changed the form and content of U.S. politics. This change is not so much the result of how the medium is used as much as the requirements, or essential nature, of the medium.

Part of the problem is that historically scholars and politicians approached political communication as simply a task of the movement of information. Audiences are viewed as targets rather than as participants. In terms of television, such a focus does not address the fundamental nature of political reality. Only by understanding television as a communication medium can the political impact be fully appreciated.

TELEVISION AS A
COMMUNICATION MEDIUM

Marshall McLuhan was the first theorist to fully recognize the impact of communication media upon society. He argued that "societies have always been shaped more by the nature of the media by which men communicate than by the content of the communication."[4] According to McLuhan, Western society has undergone four major periods of development, each of which has been characterized by the preference of one mode of mass communication over others.[5]

The first period was that of pre-literate humans. These

"tribal men" led a complex "kaleidoscopic" life receiving their information and knowledge by hearing it from others. The second period was characterized by the invention of the alphabet and the subsequent introduction of written communication. This produced a society in which the eye exceeded the ear in importance as a sensory organ. The third "revolution" occurred with the invention of moveable type and printing in the early fifteenth century. This most drastic invention changed human social, physical, and psychic lives. While we are still greatly affected by the "Gutenberg Revolution," McLuhan argues that the fourth period began as a result of the new electronic communications media. Today's electronic media encourage an acoustic rather than a visual environment, returning us once again to the "global village."

At the heart of McLuhan's argument is the now-famous notion that "the medium is the message."[6] What this means, simply, is that what we think of as the "message" is transmitted by some medium which, because of its mechanical nature, also sends a simultaneous "message." This implies that perception and interpretation of a message will be affected by the simultaneous message that is inherent in the mechanical nature of the medium. This perspective does not deny the importance of content; rather, it emphasizes the importance of the sensory ratios present in any given medium. McLuhan explains that "the extension of any one sense alters the way we think and act—the way we perceive the world . . . when ratios change, men change."[7]

The major point is that we "interact" with the media. Media becomes a pervasive environment that provides both action and reaction in a continuous fashion. This new environment encourages unification and involvement. In terms of unification, McLuhan distinguishes between the concepts of "mass" and "public." He defines the "public" as separate individuals walking around with separate, fixed points of view. The electronic media created the notion of "mass," returning us as members of the "global village," losing identity and separate action.

The various media can be described and categorized according to the degree of participation required by the audience. For McLuhan, a medium is either "hot" or "cool."[8] A "hot" medium is one that extends one single sense in "high definition," requiring little audience participation. However, a "cool" medium is of "low definition," requiring much audience participation. According to this scheme, print, radio, and film are "hot" media whereas television and telephone are "cool" media requiring extensive participation.

While these ideas are provocative and seem intuitively valid, surprisingly little empirical research has been done dealing specifically with McLuhan's ideas. Perhaps the reason for this noticeable lack of research is due to the absence of clear thought and presentation in McLuhan's works. While McLuhan emphasizes the fact that message content is of lesser importance than the medium utilized, he fails to make clear the proper relationship between content and media. Clearly a message should be designed to best utilize the uniqueness of the medium used. Implicitly, then, one should be aware of message content in terms of style, structure, etc. as it relates to the specific medium used.

In terms of "hot" and "cool," it is perhaps more useful to view the media in terms of a hierarchy. A medium is "hot" or "cool" only in relation to other media or activities. This is not a contradiction but a minor refinement. In an interview with *Playboy*, McLuhan stated that "a lecture, by the same token, is hot, but a seminar is cool; a book is hot, but a conversation or bull session is cool."[9] Thus, we can posit, that the various media from "coolest" to "hottest" would be television, film, radio, public speech, and print.

We can now begin to understand the change of political discourse as discussed in Chapter 1. Public speaking for years was "hot" because of its "print" nature as it was practiced. Speeches may be characterized by their logical, linear, step-by-step nature that reflects a "hot" literate society. "Hot" material presented over a "cool" medium does not become "cool," just "cooler." "Any political candidate," according to McLuhan, "who doesn't have such cool, low-definition qualities, which allow the viewer to fill in the gaps with his own personal identification, simply electrocutes himself on television."[10] This, McLuhan believes, happened to Richard Nixon in the 1960 presidential campaign. Nixon was "hot," presenting a high-definition, sharply defined image on television in the debates. However, in 1968, Nixon was "cool" when compared to Humphrey. "No longer the slick glib, aggressive Nixon of 1960, he had been toned down, polished, programmed and packaged into the new Nixon we saw in 1968: earnest, modest, quietly sincere—in a word, cool."[11]

There are several intriguing implications from McLuhan's notions about the media that focus on subject matter, sender of mediated messages, and the structure or nature of mediated messages. These implications, in terms of Reagan, are most interesting in comparison to the media of film.

If we accept Marshall McLuhan's characterization of television as a "cool" medium, then television is unsuited for "hot" issues or sharply defined controversial topics.

The reason is that for television, audience participation is too high. Controversial topics encourage audience unease and frustration. Television engages the viewer and demands attention. As a medium, it cannot serve as "background" as easily as radio. With television, according to McLuhan, the viewer is the screen and must "fill in the dots."[12] Film, in contrast, is "hot" and offers more data per second than television. "The viewer does not have to make the same drastic reduction of items to form his impression. He tends instead to accept the full image as a package deal."[13] With film, viewers are passive consumers of actions rather than participants in reactions. Thus, the presentation of "hot" or controversial material on television will literally force audience reaction in terms of like or dislike, favor or unfavor.

Because television is of "low definition," speech does not require the precision necessary as in theater. Television is intimate and requires a "spontaneous casualness" rather than a projected voice, character, or gesture as in film or on stage.[14]

As a medium, television is intimate, ordinary, familiar, and immediate. Viewing television is routine. The mechanism is always available. Programming is more or less continuous and its flow is contemporaneous with the flow of life. According to Tony Schwartz, constant exposure to television results in the sharing of common "TV stimuli" by everyone in society. This creates a reservoir of common media experiences that are stored in our brains. The task, therefore, is to present stimuli that "resonate" with information already stored within an individual. In effect, the message *must* conform to the medium. Mediated communication evokes meaning and each medium conditions the brain to receive and process information in specified ways. Schwartz argues that "experience with tv and radio stimuli are often more real than first-hand, face-to-face experiences."[15] In fact, he asserts that the "captured reality" of media is preferred to personal experience. In accordance with McLuhan's notions, Schwartz also argues that the key to mediated communication is that the role of audiences is altered. Instead of being targets for communication, audiences become participants. "The audience is viewed as a work force in the communication process . . ."[16]

According to John Langer, "good television personalizes whenever it can, rarely using a concept or idea without attaching it to or transforming it through the 'category of the individual'."[17] Television presents, therefore, a world of personalities who organize our reality and articulate our social agendas. Walter Cronkite's nightly statement of "And that's the way it is" to end his newscasts reinforced the certainty of his perception of the day's events. But, of course, not all personalities are right for television. For McLuhan a successful television performer must achieve a low-pressure style of presentation. In addition, "anybody whose *appearance* strongly declares his role and status in life is wrong for tv. Anybody who looks as if he might be a teacher, a doctor, a businessman, or any of a dozen other things all at the same time is right for tv."[18] The idea is that when someone looks classifiable, the viewer has nothing to fill in. Here the audience's sympathy, identification, and relation with the personality would be low.

In Hollywood, film stars are heroes, models, or even "gods." They are often described as "larger than life." Movie stars play a variety of characters, most often in extreme forms. The public wants to know "what they are really like." In contrast, television personalities are more stable and familiar. "Audiences participate," according to McLuhan, "in the inner life of the TV actor as fully as in the outer life of the movie star."[19] Fans want to see their television personalities in a role and movie stars as they really are. Contact with television personalities is frequent, movie stars sporadic. Television personalities often play themselves, movie stars play others and hide behind filmic characters. It should not surprise us, therefore, that Robert Young, who played Marcus Welby, received thousands of letters seeking medical advice or that Larry Hagman, of the television show "Dallas," is more often called J.R. in public than by his real name.

As a medium, film is similar to print. Like print, film assumes a high degree of literacy. As McLuhan observes, "the close relation, then, between the reel world of film and the private fantasy experience of the printed word is indispensable to our western acceptance of the film form."[20] We must "learn" to "read" films, to understand the pacing and shifting of perspective. Gerald Mast, noted film historian, writes, "analogous to the novel, the finished movie is not just a story, but a story told in a certain way, and it is impossible to separate what is told from how it is told. . . . the wonder is that . . . the evolution of narrative fiction can be traced back to Homer."[21] One of the films shown in the first movie theater in Paris in 1895 was of a train rushing into a railway station. The audience screamed, shouted, and ducked when it saw the train coming toward them.[22]

Finally, production techniques also contribute to the personalizing effect of television. The "close-up" is routine in television but used primarily for shock value in film. In television, the personality is more important than the storyline or plot. And television is much more interactive than film. Television viewing is social whereas film is private. Most speakers are talking directly to the audience, taking them into account rather than merely treating them as unnoticed spectators listening in from a distant position.

Technology has increased the interactive nature of television. Color increased its appeal and videotape its reality. Portable cameras, zoom lenses, and electronic equipment increase flexibility of coverage and range of shots, while graphics, split screens, etc. all contribute to a more intense interaction. In addition to intensity, the frequency of interaction has also increased. Satellite transmissions and cable news stations have increased political coverage and exposure. By spring of 1987, all announced and unannounced presidential candidates were shown daily addressing various groups. For example, the C-Span channel taped and played several times the various candidates addressing the National Mayors' Conference in the spring of 1987.

By comparing television with film, we more readily recognize the unique influences television may have upon the nature of political discourse. First, the individual or personality becomes the central structuring element for all televised political communication. Second, the medium accepts the ordinary, everyday and will reject the "special" or unusual. Third, the medium is one for reaction, not thoughtful response or reflection. Television, as a medium, is best suited for answers, not questions; solutions, not problems; and good old-fashioned "horse sense," not wisdom. Finally, our definition of audience must change. The term "viewers" implies individual choice and action, unlike the term "mass." In the days before television, members of the public sought an audience with the leaders of a nation. Today, the leaders actively seek an audience with us, in our living rooms. The audience has the control. The true political power of the public no longer resides in the ballot or vote but in the controls of the television.

PRESIDENTIAL POLITICS IN THE TELEVISION AGE

The media have stimulated a fundamental change in the nature and structure of political content, organization, and style. Political historian Theodore White proclaimed in a public lecture in 1985 that "all American politics today are videotropic. Every candidate turns or pitches his entire campaign to the sum of television."[23] The nature and structure of the media dictate the nature and structure of U.S. politics. And television is the supreme medium of impact and attention. Joshua Meyrowitz provides an interesting example. When the president and his wife meet with an interviewer, is it an intimate social meeting among three people or is it a public performance before the nation? For Meyrowitz it is both which makes it neither. "To the extent that actions are shaped to fit particular social settings, this new setting leads to new actions and new social meanings. . . . We have not only a different situation, but also a different president, and—in the long run—a different presidency."[24]

It is useful to go beyond theoretical implications and to identify specific influences of television upon presidential politics. Television impacts the nature of political information, the "type" and behavior of politicians, and the nature of citizen political participation.

Political Information

Television news is the prime source of information for the public. The electorate receives 65 percent of its political information through television programming.[25] The news on television is more believable, exciting, and dramatic than in other media. Thus, the portrayal of the nightly news is the single most important element in impacting political cognitions in America.

News became politically important in 1963 when networks increased the evening news programs from 15 minutes to a half-hour format. Their importance also increased during the 1960s with Kennedy's assassination, civil rights protests, and the Vietnam War. These events provided dramatic material for journalists. Television, while national in scope, became a local medium. World events were happening in the "backyards" of Americans. Television became much more political in coverage than newspapers, and human interest stories were dramatic, usually focusing on political figures. In short, television news nationalized and politicized stories.

The result of this transformation of the role of the media in American politics, according to Dan Nimmo and James Combs, is that few people learn about politics from direct experience.[26] They argue that political realities are mediated through mass and group communication. The result is the "creation, transmission, and adoption of political fantasies as realistic views of what takes place."[27] They define fantasy as "a credible picture of the world that is created when one interprets mediated experiences as the way things are and takes for granted the authenticity of the mediated reality without checking against alternative, perhaps contradictory, realities so long as the fantasy offers dramatic proof for one's expectations."[28] Thus, the fantasy does not need to be true but believable. From Nimmo and Combs's perspective, television news is storytelling and employs the elements of the dramatic narrative, utilizing verbal and nonverbal symbols, sound, and visual imagery. The key, then, is not so much in creating good, one-shot campaign ads, but in learning the artful manipulation of television news. This act is what Martin Schram refers to as the greatest of "America's video games."[29]

Because of the demands of the medium, television journalism must be entertaining and highly visual. News crews, therefore, trim stories to support film and visual elements. The film footage no longer is used to illustrate stories but is used to tell the story.[30] This means that the footage stands alone with little or no perspective or analysis. Peter Jennings, anchor for ABC's *World News Tonight*, states that "television is afraid of being dull . . . in television, you're obligated to write to the pictures."[31] Lane Vernardos, executive producer of *The CBS Evening News With Dan Rather*, builds news stories around exciting video rather than the strongest hard news stories.[32] Today, many news stories are prepared in advance. Producers develop a story angle and send reporters to capture the story on film. Because of economic factors, news crews don't want to waste footage and are more likely to stay near the Washington and New York areas.

The fact of the matter is that the news industry looks for and shares "news that wiggles." However, the more indepth the coverage the less "wiggle." Thus, the elements of action and movement are stressed over more cognitive elements. Emotional responses are the ones the public remembers and help define future reactions to people and events.

In accordance to television's need to personalize, the individual anchors and reporters have increased in importance. The reporters have become part of the story rather than just providing an overview or orientation. The narrative style of television makes it personal and credible. Many of the "contrived" interviews appear spontaneous and give the appearance of looking through the window of reality viewing "real" people and "real" events. It is the "shading" of public perceptions and the weighing of public issues that give the media power.

Television is not suited for the presentation or discussion of complex issues and policies. Stephen Wayne reports that in 1980, CBS News spent only 20 to 25 percent of their presidential election coverage on issues.[33] The media prefer to deal in dichotomies—win or lose, right or wrong, good or bad. As John Chancellor, former anchor of NBC's *Evening News* observes, "television is very good at conveying experience, and not very good at conveying facts."[34] Television is a sales medium, best at presenting a dynamic message in the simplest form possible.

It is this issue of television's failure to properly inform and educate the public on political matters that frustrates most political scholars. Jorol Manheim ponders the question "Can democracy survive television?" For him, as the public becomes even more reliant upon television as a source of political information and the medium increasingly simplifies the information, the ability to recognize, perform, and appreciate complex social issues will also decline. The result "will be a continuing qualitative reduction of the intellectual content of political discourse among the mass of American citizens which may enable an elite which preserves the requisite knowledge, skills, and resources more effectively to manipulate the polity."[35]

The fact is that there is a great deal of difference in how events are reported on television as compared to other media. On television, the news tends to be more political, personal, and critical than on other media. Television demands drama and a visual slice of life rather than comprehensive coverage of life, people, and events.

In terms of media dissemination of political communication, Schram concluded his study by stating that "for all their innovative new graphics, for all their chroma-key computers, for all of their sophisticated satellites, their high-tech and lofty intentions, America's television networks really did not take one giant step for mankind, in explaining the issues of 1984 to the voters."[36]

Politicians

According to Meyrowtiz, electronic media affected social hierarchy in two ways.[37] First, the media changed the required skills of leaders. Media knowledge impacts everything from how to speak to what to wear. Second, the media changed the balance of power between leaders and followers. Television provides the "appearance" of accessibility to national leaders. Leaders can be challenged. All information is public and has a right to be shared. As we become more familiar with leaders, we question their status and bases for "superiority." The more we truly know our leaders, the less "great" they can be.

The solution to this paradox, of course, is for our leaders to become media celebrities or personalities. A celebrity is a "human pseudo-event," in which people are "known for their well-knownness."[38] Nimmo and Combs argue that celebrities are fantasies—better than "normal" people in looks, brains, and social skills. They live in a world of excitement, drama, and mystery. We need celebrities as much as they need us. We come to know them through the media. We participate vicariously in their drama through "artificial interactions." Political celebrities have numerous advantages, such as name recognition, fundraising, and perceived power, to name only a few. Politicians, therefore, must simply study the art of self-promotion in order to become celebrity, fantasy figures.

An essential part of the process, of course, is nurturing the proper image, persona, or personality. It is human nature to reduce the complexity of our world and formulate convenient preestablished categories of factors and characteristics. In accordance with Schwartz's notions, we make inferences about politicians based not on objective experience but on previous stored knowledge, likes, dislikes, etc. Television especially encourages focus upon personalities rather than abstract issues. Personalities, as already discussed, are more salient and easier to understand than issues. Most research also shows that there is a great deal of stability in citizen criteria for presidential and candidate personalities.[39] This symbiotic relationship is demonstrated in a study by Rodger Streitmatter on the impact of presidential personality on news coverage. He found that a president receives 50 percent more coverage if the personality is robust and outgoing, appealing to both the public and journalists.[40]

For candidates, the process is rather easy. Pollsters identify the desired qualities and candidates act accordingly. Candidates, of course, need the help of media and polling professionals to help project the desired image to the public.

The most prevalent type of appeal found in television political commercials is the "benevolent leader."[41]

Benevolent leader appeals focus on personality traits rather than policy or programmatic issues. The goal is to develop a correspondence between role expectations for a public office and the persona of the candidate. Ad makers tend to favor the traits of compassion, empathy, integrity, activity, strength, and knowledge. Their ads encourage the electorate to thus view elections as choices between people and personalities rather than issues.

As mentioned earlier, camera angles can enhance emotional appeals. Close-ups produce a warm, intimate image, calling attention to detail, and create more emotional involvement. Low camera angles contribute to perceptions of strength, dominance, importance, and potency. High camera angles (i.e., top to bottom) imply weakness. To increase excitement, political ads use quick cuts to heighten the sense of action and tension, and to confirm expectations of candidate dynamism.[42]

The most comprehensive and systematic study of television's impact upon presidential discourse is Roderick Hart's *Verbal Style and the Presidency*. "Television," Hart argues, "gives us a one-dimensional presidency. It presents our presidents to us in their Sunday best but without their souls or feelings."[43] He found that on television presidential speech contains less self-references and more familiarity, human interest, and optimism than in live settings. This means that presidents are more personal with live audiences. Television demands careful, proper presentations in both words and visuals. Ironically, what made Lyndon Johnson a great politician caused him problems in the media age as president. Jim Heath remembers that "although in small groups he could mesmerize listeners with his commanding presence and endless string of anecdotes and political fables, when he spoke to

large gatherings or on radio and tv he was dull, uninspir-
ing, and—to some—flatly unpleasant."[44] Doris Kearns
claims that Johnson's fear of making grammatical or syn-
tactical mistakes made him stick close to speech texts, thus
making him even more rigid.[45]

For politicians, television has created a short-term
political environment. The reactive nature of the medium
makes it too costly to endorse long-term, controversial
policies. Leaders, candidates, and administrators must
adapt in political form and content to the demands of
television. These demands will be discussed in greater
detail in the next chapter.

Nature of Political Participation

There are two basic issues at the heart of most political
inquiry. The first is how does the element of study influence the type or quality of leadership. This book focuses
on that issue. The second question deals with the "quality"
of democracy in the United States. Does our electoral process encourage democracy? A cursory analysis would appear to support the notion that television is a valuable tool
for democratic rule. It exposes candidates to all people and
encourages singular, national rather than regional
responses to major questions and issues. In short, television keeps the candidates "honest."

I, however, am not as optimistic about the role of television in electoral politics. At the very least, television has
altered the nature of political participation in the United
States and thus the "quality" of democratic government.
Although television is highly involving, it does not encourage critical involvement of information. The medium
literally reduces the message and prepares the viewer for

its nearly automatic reception. This process is similar to consuming a great deal of food of little nutritional value. The meal is satisfying but critically deficient. Humans fear isolation and television provides a pressure to conform; responses become as predictable as those to the bell of Pavlov's dog. Television, then, is an individual medium that produces mass responses.

The concern here is not so much for political campaigns because, to use the above analogy, the public knows that the meals are primarily "desserts." The concern is for non-election years when the salience for political messages is low and the risk for manipulation is high. Attitudes can be more easily changed or altered in non-election years than during the heat of a campaign. Television news becomes the vehicle for political issue formation and attitude alteration. Television, therefore, has caused a greater impact of the press on political decision making. Because viewers internalize stories, the stories become persuasive. The daily presentations become the framework for individual responses and future reactions. In terms of agenda setting, Shanto Iyenzar and Donald Kinder found that television news alters the public's sense of national priorities, and coverage of a particular problem tends to be more powerful among people affected. They also found that the lead stories of the broadcasts are most memorable.[46] Thus, as already noted, the politicians who can control and dominate television coverage will have the best opportunity to espouse their views and garner support.

Finally, our primary system was made for television. It has drama, excitement, winners, and losers. The coverage of the early primaries makes a national trend out of the results. Candidates become contenders and public opinion polls become the benchmark for success.

Television has probably made us politically lazy. Consciously watching the news and following the polls may satisfy our appetites but does little in making the public proactive rather than reactive. Two-way, interactive television may be a step toward direct democracy, but I doubt it would improve the quality of citizen participation.

CONCLUSION

There is little doubt or disagreement that television has changed the fundamental nature of U.S. politics. Television has impacted the nature of issues, the form of citizen participation, and the kind of people who are elected. To be successful simply means proper adaptation to the medium. First, the medium requires special adaptation of the message. It needs to be simple, dramatic, and involving. Second, the medium requires a unique structure. Its contents must revolve around a person, a single individual who gives the message context and meaning. For politicians, the implications are clear. Focus on the person—not the issues. Control visual images, stories, and news reports to project the proper persona. The result is a predictable public response. To this end, Ronald Reagan is king. Ronald Reagan is the first to operationalize McLuhan's notion of "the medium is the message."

NOTES

1. Aristotle, *Politics* (Edited and translated by Ernest Barker) (New York: Oxford University Press, 1970), p. 292.
2. Edwin Diamond and Stephen Bates, *The Spot* (Cambridge, MA: MIT Press, 1984), p. 76.

3. Marshall McLuhan and Quentin Fiore, *The Medium is the Message* (New York: Bantam Books, 1967), p. 76.

4. McLuhan and Fiore, *Medium is the Message,* p. 8.

5. See Marshall McLuhan, *Understanding Media* (New York: New American Library, 1964) and McLuhan and Fiore, *Medium is the Message.*

6. See McLuhan and Fiore, *Medium is the Message.*

7. McLuhan and Fiore, *Medium is the Message,* pp. 41 and 47.

8. See McLuhan, *Understanding Media.*

9. "Playboy Interview: Marshall McLuhan," *Playboy Magazine,* March, 1969, p. 61.

10. "Playboy Interview," p. 61.

11. "Playboy Interview," p. 62.

12. McLuhan, *Understanding Media,* p. 272.

13. McLuhan, *Understanding Media,* p. 273.

14. McLuhan, *Understanding Media,* pp. 176-182.

15. Tony Schwartz, *The Responsive Chord* (New York: Anchor Books, 1973), p. 44.

16. Schwartz, *Responsive Chord,* p. 44.

17. John Langer, "Television's 'Personality System'," *Media, Culture and Society,* vol. 4, 1981, p. 352.

18. McLuhan, *Understanding Media,* p. 288.

19. McLuhan, *Understanding Media,* p. 276.

20. McLuhan, *Understanding Media,* p. 250.

21. Gerald Mast, *A Short History of the Movies* (Indianapolis, IN: Pegasus, 1971), p. 9.

22. Mast, *Short History,* pp. 32-33.

23. As quoted in Martin Schram, *The Great American Video Game* (New York: William Morrow & Co., 1987), p. 16.

24. Joshua Meyrowitz, *No Sense of Place* (New York: Oxford University Press, 1985), p. 43.

25. Lynda Kaid and Dorothy Davidson, "Elements of Videostyle" in *New Perspectives on Political Advertising,* Lynda Kaid, Dan Nimmo, and Keith Sanders, eds. (Carbondale, IL: Southern Illinois University Press, 1986), p. 185.

26. See Dan Nimmo and James Combs, *Mediated Political Realities* (New York: Longman, 1983).

27. Nimmo and Combs, *Mediated Political Realities,* p. xv.

28. Nimmo and Combs, *Mediated Political Realities,* p. 8.

29. Schram, *Great American Video Game,* p. 28.

30. David Altheide and Robert Snow, *Media Logic* (Beverly Hills, CA: Sage, 1979), pp. 109-110.

31. As quoted in Schram, *Great American Video Game,* p. 58.

32. As reported in Schram, *Great American Video Game,* p. 51.

33. Stephen Wayne, *The Road to the White House,* 2nd. ed. (New York: St. Martin's Press, 1984), p. 228.

34. As quoted in Schram, *Great American Video Game,* p. 52.

35. Jorol Manheim, "Can Democracy Survive Television?" in *Media Power in Politics,* Doris Graber, ed. (Washington, D.C.: Congressional Quarterly, Inc., 1984), p. 134.

36. Schram, *Great American Video Game,* p. 287.

37. Meyrowitz, *No Sense of Place,* p. 161.

38. Nimmo and Combs, *Mediated Political Realities,* p. 93.

39. Arthur Miller et al., "Cognitive Representations of Candidate Assessments" in *Political Communication Yearbook 1984,* Keith Sanders, Lynda Kaid, and Dan Nimmo, eds. (Carbondale, IL: Southern Illinois University Press, 1985), p. 191.

40. Rodger Streitmatter, "The Impact of Presidential Personality on News Coverage in Major Newspapers," *Journalism Quarterly,* Spring 1985, pp. 66-73.

41. Richard Joslyn, "Political Advertising and the Meaning of Elections" in *New Perspectives on Political Advertising,* Lynda Kaid, Dan Nimmo, and Keith Sanders, eds. (Carbondale, IL: Southern Illinois University Press, 1986), p. 179.

42. Kaid and Davidson, *New Perspectives,* pp. 189-190.

43. Roderick Hart, *Verbal Style and the Presidency* (Orlando, FL: Academic Press, 1984), p. 54.

44. As quoted in Hart, *Verbal Style,* p. 113.

45. Doris Kearns, *Lyndon Johnson and the American Dream* (New York: Harper & Row, 1976), p. 318.

46. Shanto Iyenzar and Donald Kinder, "Psychological Accounts of Agenda-Setting" in *Mass Media and Political Thought,* Sidney Kraus and Richard Perloff, eds. (Beverly Hills, CA: Sage, 1985), p. 133.

4
The Primetime Presidency of Ronald Reagan

The argument presented thus far is that we have entered a new age of presidential politics. The medium of television has become the primary medium and tool of both campaigning and governing. From 1949 to 1956, homes with at least one television increased from one million to thirty-five million. By 1960, television was overwhelmingly perceived as the most important source of information. And just eight years later, television surpassed newspapers in terms of trustworthiness.[1] As a result, the nature of the contemporary presidency is directly linked to the evolution of television. The Reagan revolution is not so much in ideology or programs but in instituting the primetime presidency.

There are three critical dimensions to the primetime presidency. First, the message must fit the medium in both form and content. Second, industry demands for news must be carefully crafted by the incumbent. Finally, today's president must be, if not an actor, at least a "media celebrity." These dimensions will become clear upon analysis.

"THE MEDIUM IS THE MESSAGE"

Although less theoretical or philosophical than McLuhan, the notion that "the medium is the message" recognizes the fact that a message must conform in terms of content and structure to a medium in order to maximize impact and effectiveness. Reagan's cool, laid-back style is perfect for television. As previously stated, television rejects intense, "hot," and controversial material. Reagan was able to literally step through the television and join Americans in their living rooms in discussing the state of the nation. The consequence of this ability, according to Martin Schram, is that "Americans came to understand that if they were happy with Reagan's policies, the president deserved the credit, and if they were unhappy with them, the president was there with them, plainly disgusted too."[2]

The themes of the Reagan presidency have been heroism, faith, and patriotism. In Reagan's inauguration of 1981, he set forth his beliefs that America has a special mission to the world, that individual action is superior to governmental action, and that governments threaten individual liberty. Reagan's primetime presidency offers positive and idealized images. As president, he identifies and welcomes heroes, espouses faith in God and country, and surrounds himself with icons of patriotism. By the reelection of 1984, the advertisers who had produced Pepsi commercials brought their skills to Reagan the product. The spots proclaimed that "It's morning again in America," showing a wedding, a family moving into a new home, fertile fields, and employed construction workers. The anthem in the spots stated in part:

I'm proud to be an American, Where at least I know I'm free; And I won't forget the men who died who gave that flag to me; And I'll gladly stand up—next to you—and defend her still today, 'Cause there ain't no doubt I love this land; God bless the U.S.A.!

By the summer of 1984, we saw Reagan meet with troops in Korea, veterans of World War II in Normandy, Olympic heroes, widows of fallen American soldiers, and citizens on Labor Day and beside the Statue of Liberty. In contrast, Mondale proclaimed the doom of high deficits, nuclear war, and the plight of the elderly. In terms of the campaign, Dan Rather concludes that "the Reagan people saw the whole campaign as a movie. . . . the Mondale people—at best—saw it as a series of quick sound bites."[3]

Roderick Hart's microscopic analysis of Reagan's rhetoric identifies three special characteristics.[4] First, Reagan's rhetoric provides a sense of momentum—an emotional, take-charge, can-do spirit of optimism that deals with broad statements of philosophy rather than of policy. Second, Reagan's rhetoric identifies a clear "sense of place," describing who we are, what's on our minds, and what we should do, and does so in short, crisp sentences with little embellishment. This allows him to gloss over unpleasant facts, reduce complex issues, and create mass appeal. As Hart observes, "his words never force his listeners to imagine things they are incapable of imagining or require that they make a taxing intellectual association. . . . His language is drawn from life as it is lived most simply."[5] Finally, whereas Carter provided a sense of morality, Reagan provides a strong sense of tradition. His public addresses are national celebrations complete with appropriate national symbols and ceremonial settings.

Reagan's idealized images and cheerleader role are perfect for television. In his stories, Reagan changes reality to make it uplifting and positive. Once, for example, Reagan told of a football game in which the team won in the last twenty seconds primarily because of his key block. In real life, he missed his block, but upon the re-creation he made it. Reagan turns real-life failure to success, which is much more dramatic and heroic, for television.[6] In over 50 films, Reagan only once played the heavy—a role that would be rejected on television. Film invites viewers to observe forbidden acts from a distance—a distance that keeps us "clean." Television, as a medium, does not allow a protective distance. Because of the interactive nature of television, we become partners in the sharing of bad news and events. To stay "clean," audiences must actively disassociate themselves from bad messages and reject the sources. Doomsayers are often tragic heroes in film but certainly villains on television.

On the eve of his 1980 victory, when asked what the electorate see in him, Reagan responded, "I think maybe they see themselves and that I'm one of them."[7] His rhetorical style is not flamboyant, but simple, and expresses the thoughts of common Americans. Reagan wrote most of his final speeches. He would shorten sentences and simplify images so that the average citizen would readily understand. Reagan knows how to write for the ear rather than the eye, a reason why so many of his speeches sound better than they read. This style, again, is best for television and increases his acceptance. Reagan makes a virtue of acting as if he doesn't know more than the voters. In our homes, Reagan appears as an informed equal, a reflection of us rather than a superior, star individual. Yet, Garry Wills reports that "Reagan has often 'goofed' to look more natural—broken the grammar of sentences, feigned embarrassment, professionally avoided the appearance of being a professional. It is an important art in democratic politics."[8] On television, we relate to the human characters who are imperfect and laid back, and show a sense of humor. Reagan talks with an audience, not at them. His appearance does not declare his role and status.

Reagan seldom acts; others in his administration do that. But Reagan shares much reaction to events, people, and issues. He can get angry when pushed too far, recognize a woman reporter at a press conference simply because she wears a red dress, Nancy's favorite color, or even berate Russia, but does so in the tone and voice of Marcus Welby telling a sick patient to "shape up or else." Reagan certainly takes a stand but does so with humility, righteousness, and anecdotes and quotes from letters written by children or common, everyday American heroes. He tells stories to make his points. As Joshua Meyrowitz observes, "if Nixon was thesis and Carter antithesis, then Reagan is synthesis. He is a man who says he will 'talk Tough,' but does so in a soft-spoken, folksy style. He seems comfortable in a full spectrum of costumes, from tuxedos to cowboy suits, and in a wide range of activities from ballroom dancing to gardening. He is part Nixon, part Carter, an 'imperial' president who chops his own wood. Unlike Nixon, Reagan appears to be a sweet and likable person; unlike Carter, he offers a romantic notion of America's power and destiny."[9]

Not only is the content of Reagan's messages right for television but so is the structure or form of the messages. Even in Reagan's most straightforward addresses before

Congress, he creates a sense of drama through relating stories and parables. According to Paul Erickson, these parables contain all the elements of fiction: distinctive characters, settings, plot, theme or moral, and a narrative point of view.[10] Although identified by name, the characters are historic and symbolic, reflecting the values of family, patriotism, tradition, freedom, faith, etc. A single hero mobilizes strong emotions. Even with real, genuine stories he makes complex operations the story of one person.

In addition to the personalized story, Reagan carefully controls the settings and backdrops to heighten the dramatic effect. The perfect example is the June 6, 1984 ceremony of Normandy. He reduced the invasion to one man, Private Zanatta, whose daughter had vowed to attend the ceremony in his absence. For Sam Donaldson, the ceremony was the epitome of theatrical news management. Reagan's performance included beautiful scenery (flags, a bluff overlooking a beach, blue sea) and human emotion (aged heroes, tears). Donaldson, although recognizing the staging of the event, admits, "I put three pounds of it in because it was a compelling, dramatic moment."[11] "By personifying his beliefs about good and evil in simply drawn men and women," Erickson argues that the "president provides points of reference and points of view for his audience."[12] Thus, the characters are tools suited for the media. Garry Wills concurs by observing that Reagan "renews our past by resuming it. His approach is not discoursive, setting up sequences of time or thought, but associative; not a tracking shot, but montage. We make the connections."[13] Such an approach maximizes individual participation and interaction.

As noted in the last chapter, television personalizes whenever it can and Reagan has perfected the "politics of individualism."[14] Bert Rockman argues that there is a predisposition in the United States toward personalism in politics that is rooted in our history, culture, and institutions.[15] Our political system promotes individual entrepreneurship where leadership, regardless of context, is an individual quest. Corporations are structured with the focus on individual responsibility rather than collective responsibility. Thus, by personalizing the office and issues, Reagan complements the requirements of the form and content of the television medium.

GOVERNING THROUGH THE DAILY NEWS

Today, political competence encompasses not only performance but the elements of personality, image, and style. Political rituals have replaced doctrine in U.S. politics and it has always been important to manage the medium of the era. For example, Meyrowitz argues that "film allowed a short Wilson to appear tall, just as radio permitted a disabled Franklin Roosevelt to sound powerful, and television allowed a young Kennedy to look self-assured and experienced."[16] Reagan not only used television to present a positive, desired image but to govern the nation.

Reagan's staff, as media professionals, recognized that the public has less and less of a historical memory. This requires a daily concern rather than a long-term perspective for impression management. They also recognized that the mass media expected a steady and constant "din" from the White House. And, as Hart confirmed in a recent study, just "talking" provides a president with media access and coverage.[17] Finally, the staff knew that television could be managed because of what Gerald Pomper refers to as its limitation: "Reporters can comment only in the context of a picture; the medium is impotent without 'photo opportunities' and cannot easily resist a story with good visual possibilities."[18]

As a result, Martin Schram argues that "night after night, Reagan had his way with the television news. He had succeeded in setting their agenda and framing their stories by posing for the cameras in one beautiful and compelling setting after another."[19] The key, therefore, was not to control what the news correspondents would be saying but to control what America was seeing.

Lesley Stahl, CBS News White House correspondent, was one of the first to attempt to tell the American people that Ronald Reagan's television access and presence was well orchestrated but actually contradicted policy positions. While presenting this viewpoint, the video showed Reagan with handicapped Olympians, at a senior citizen housing project, at home riding horses and cutting wood, in visions from Normany, with the Vietnam Unknown Soldier, and comforting families of dead marines. While the verbal report was critical and negative, the visual was positive and reinforced the values espoused by Reagan for years. A member of Reagan's staff was actually pleased with the piece. "We're in the middle of a campaign and you gave us four-and-a-half minutes of great pictures of Ronald Reagan . . . and that's all the American people see."[20] The point is that the pictures tell the story more than the verbiage. Television, as "cool," requires the viewer to participate in the generally positive "Americana" experiences. In effect, the viewers were sharing them (and in some cases sharing them for a second or third time) with Reagan.

The strategy for exposure was clear. The daily priorities were: network evening news, morning shows, Cable News Network, and local regional news programs.[21] Details of the daily nature of government, policy, and foreign affairs were avoided. Photo opportunities were granted with no questions allowed. Press briefings were held late in the day, reducing time for network editing. News outlets outside Washington were developed. In fact, in Reagan's first three years, he gave the press 194 interviews and 150 special White House briefings from outside Washington.

The lesson is clear. Maintaining popular support means carefully controlling what is seen rather than what is said. To govern the nation means controlling the videos in the evening news.

RONALD REAGAN AND THE TELEVISION PERSONALITY

Martin Kaplan, Mondale's speechwriter, said rather facetiously the day after the 1984 election that the only candidate who could have beaten "old actor Reagan" was another actor or a television anchorman, such as Robert Redford or Walter Cronkite.[22] But Reagan's success is more than just being an "old actor." Hart characterizes him as "combination orator-rhetorician-leader and performer"—a television performer.[23]

My central argument is that what makes Ronald Reagan successful on television is actually what prevented him from being a true movie star. Reagan has not used television as much as he has adapted to its essential requirements as a medium. In short, Reagan is a much better actor as president on television than he ever was in Hollywood. As an actor, his success was switching from the "big screen" of films to the "small screen" of television. Michael Rogin best summarizes the argument by observing that a failure in Hollywood succeeds in politics by breaking down the disjunction between image and life more effectively than the bigger-than-life stars of movies.[24]

If we think of some very successful television stars, Fred MacMurray, Bob Newhart, James Garner to name only a few, we see that they are really "smaller than life." Their reactions tend to diminish the various events or situations in which they find themselves. Intense emotions are manageable. Their qualities are soothing, attractive, and everyday.

Ronald Reagan is simply a television personality. His manner of communication fits the requirements of television as a medium—not necessarily those of governing or ruling a nation. Reagan, through the medium of television, maximizes Kenneth Burke's concept of identification. Indeed, Reagan truly reinforces the myth that any citizen can become president of the United States. But he does so because he is a *television* actor. Although truly radical, Ronald Reagan appears passive and "cool."

Reagan has long favored and recognized the power of television as a medium. In *Where's the Rest of Me?*, he claims to be "one of the first established motion picture stars deliberately to choose it for my own field at a time when everyone of stature in Hollywood was delicately holding their noses about it."[25] He writes, "I do not think [television] represents a new medium; it is, instead, simply a new kind of theatre. It is the proscenium arch in miniature brought into the home."[26] Movies, Reagan argues, offered an emotional experience once a week or so but now television "is a knob within easy reach seven nights a week."[27] According to Ted Koppel of ABC News, Reagan moved effortlessly from radio to movies, from movies to television, and by the mid-60s, television had proved itself to be the most effective selling medium of all time.[28]

Reagan's philosophy of acting is also well suited to the medium of television. Reagan claims an actor learns to see himself as others see him, from the outside in rather than the inside out.[29] He recalls that his high school drama teacher "had the knack of quietly leading us into a performance, of making us think our roles instead of acting them out mechanically."[30] It is this audience perspective that is critical on successful television performances that result in audience participation and identification. On stage, there is the willing suspension of disbelief between the audience and actors that is not the case on television. Reagan believes that the basis of the dramatic form of entertainment is "the emotional catharsis experienced by the audience."[31]

Reagan clearly possesses skills that enable him to project ideas to audiences both in person and through the media. This ability stems from what Hart calls "semantic egalitarianism," the belief that "no philosophical concept is so subtle that it cannot be turned into a political slogan."[32] Reagan became a good listener while touring for General Electric. He made notes of successful lines, phrases, and jokes.[33] Reagan's years in radio greatly aided in the development of his language and vocal skills. These skills allow Reagan to establish an emotional link with audiences. Reagan told Lou Cannon in an interview that "the secret of announcing is to make reading sound like talking."[34] He prefers to rehearse passages out loud so the words will sound spontaneous. Cannon concludes that Reagan's natural-sounding delivery is no accident and is the result of hard work and careful preparation. His delivery, too, fits best with television. "He does not overaccent his lines, but underplays them, letting just enough vibrancy enter his voice not to be dull. This easiness," according to Garry Wills, "is what kept him from some intense roles he aspired to; but it was his protection as well."[35] And finally, Reagan's radio days of reconstructing ballgames encouraged the notion that drama mattered more than accuracy. In fact, he made some games sound more exciting than the real thing. Reagan brags of countless flyballs he had to create while waiting for game information over the wire services.[36] For Richard Schickel, "Reagan's fictive embroidery did not distort the account of the game as it progressed—the hits, misses, and errors were all present and accounted for—and the rest was just entertainment."[37] The result, as already noted, is the remarkable talent of creating and telling stories that touch the human heart and spirit.

Ronald Reagan's simplified, idealistic view of the world also plays well on television. A good performer loves to please the audience, but beyond that is the fact that Reagan believes in what he says. "With Reagan," Wills argues, "perfection of the pretense lies in the fact that he does not know he is pretending. He believes the individualist myths that help him play his communal role . . . a perfect blend of an authentic America he grew up in and of that America's own fables about its past."[38] In his heart, Reagan is a salesman who believes in his product—Ronald Reagan. He can project himself into fantastic narratives and turn personal history into, although fiction, at least heroic fiction. This results from Reagan's inability to transform himself through art. Schickel concludes that because Reagan lacked the "gift of transcendence," acting could only provide an extension of reality rather than an escape from it.[39] Michael Rogin's central argument in *Ronald Reagan, The Movie* is that Reagan found out who he was through the roles he played on film, thus merging his onscreen and offscreen identities.[40] The problem is that when Reagan shifts from film to reality, he casts reality in terms of make-believe.

Writers and critics claim that Reagan is not a very good "professional" actor.[41] Criticisms include distorted facial expressions, wooden gestures, lack of intensity, and lack of getting into character. "He never aspired to become the character he played. . . . He always acted like Ronald Reagan. It is a heartwarming role."[42] But this insistence upon playing himself is what allowed Reagan to succeed. Schickel argues that Reagan succeeded as an actor "precisely because he refused to act, in the general sense of the word. He refused to try to impose himself on events, to shape them to his uses."[43] Wills concurs by observing that "Ronald Reagan is old and young—an actor, but with only one role. Because he acts himself, we know he is authentic. A professional, he is always the amateur."[44]

From the earlier discussion of the television medium, it is easy to see that while Reagan may be a poor film actor, he is a very good television actor. His style matches the requirements of the television medium. He is, to put it simply, a character actor who is comfortable within a defined (and controlled) context. Even in the 1980 presidential campaign it was a priority of the Reagan staff to make the candidate "stick to the script."[45] Reagan had a weakness for making extemporaneous and rather careless political remarks. Accuracy was less important than the point to be made. He would accept anything read or heard as fact and consider it worthy if it supported a position, and would restate it in compelling settings and dramatic form.

In television, like Hollywood, the perfect technique is imperceptible. The medium provides techniques to make persuasion look nonpersuasive. For the camera, the scenes look unstaged and Reagan acted as a non-actor—a very challenging role for any actor. Careful analysis provides several patterned responses of Reagan that evoke audience emotion. For example, Wills describes Reagan's "choreography of candor" as: " 'Well'—eyes down, eyes up, smile, slight dip of head to the right, and begin . . ."[46]

For Ronald Reagan, the essence of political success comes from expressing how people feel—not by expressing what they think. Bernard Frazer, Reagan's former drama coach, recognized this ability. "He expressed people's feelings, you see, in words. He was good at that particular thing."[47] And Reagan also recognizes the power of expressing how people feel. In his welcome to the 1981 Academy Awards, Reagan said, "It is the motion picture that shows all of us not only how we look and sound but—more importantly—how we feel."[48] The personalizing medium of television allows the actor in the proper setting to engage us and become part of us in defining the world. Ronald Reagan "The Great Communicator" is really Ronald Reagan the "great television communicator."

CONCLUSION

Ronald Reagan is our first true television president. His persona, messages, and behavior fit the medium's requirements in terms of form, content, and industry demands. Reagan surrounds himself with professionals of the modern communications technology. They make sure the settings are correct and the messages clear. Reagan as a television actor delivers the lines and gestures to ensure the desired response—agreement through empathy. Dramatic expressions mix reality with fantasy, who we think we are with whom we want to be, and the world as it is with the world as it should be. To lead is not to be led. To lead is not to manage. To lead is to mirror ourselves.

Through snapshots we validate who we are and what we did. We construct the narratives, correct our wrongs, and celebrate the good times. Events we photograph we control. Each photo we take has a purpose, a meaning. Reagan provides action photographs that are positive, optimistic, and even heroic. Television is a medium for social expression, not social action.

NOTES

1. Richard Rubin, *Press, Party, and Presidency* (New York: W. W. Norton, 1981), p. 148.

2. Martin Schram, *The Great American Video Game* (New York: William Morrow & Co., 1987), p. 26.

3. As quoted in Schram, *Great American Video Game*, p. 59.

4. Roderick Hart, *Verbal Style and the Presidency* (Orlando, FL: Academic Press, 1984), pp. 215-228.

5. Hart, *Verbal Style*, p. 224.

6. Michael Rogin, *Ronald Reagan, The Movie* (Beverly Hills, CA: University of California Press, 1987), p. 14.

7. Rogin, *Ronald Reagan*, p. 12.

8. Garry Wills, *Reagan's America* (New York: Doubleday, 1987), p. 163.

9. Joshua Meyrowitz, *No Sense of Place* (New York: Oxford University Press, 1985), p. 301.

10. Paul Erickson, *Reagan Speaks* (New York: New York University Press, 1985), p. 6.

11. Schram, *Great American Video Game,* p. 63.

12. Schram, *Great American Video Game,* p. 51.

13. Wills, *Reagan's America,* p. 4.

14. See Richard Reeves, *The Reagan Detour* (New York: Simon & Schuster, 1985), pp. 93-107.

15. Bert Rockman, *The Leadership Question* (New York: Praeger, 1984), pp. 177-178.

16. Meyrowitz, *No Sense of Place,* p. 281.

17. Roderick Hart, *The Sound of Leadership* (Chicago: University of Chicago Press, 1987), pp. 32-39.

18. Gerald Pomper et al., *The Election of 1984* (Chatham, NJ: Chatham House Publishers, 1985), p. 162.

19. Schram, *Great American Video Game,* p. 23.

20. Schram, *Great American Video Game,* p. 26.

21. Samuel Kernell, *Going Public* (Washington, D.C.: Congressional Quarterly Press, 1986), pp. 74-75.

22. Reeves, *Reagan Detour,* pp. 93-94.

23. Hart, *Verbal Style,* p. 214.

24. Rogin, *Ronald Reagan,* p. 38.

25. Ronald Reagan with Richard Huber, *Where's the Rest of Me?* (New York: Dell edition, 1981), p. 263.

26. Reagan, *Where's the Rest of Me?,* p. 333.

27. Reagan, *Where's the Rest of Me?* p. 334.

28. "Jennings Koppel Report: Memo to the Future", ABC News, April 23, 1987, transcript, p. 5.

29. Reagan, *Where's the Rest of Me?,* p. 79.

30. Reagan, *Where's the Rest of Me?,* p. 47.

31. Reagan, *Where's the Rest of Me?,* p. 334.

32. Hart, *Verbal Style,* p. 233.

33. Lou Cannon, *Reagan* (New York: Putnam, 1982), pp. 93-94.

34. Cannon, *Reagan,* p. 45.

35. Wills, *Reagan's America,* p. 136.

36. See Wills, *Reagan's America,* p. 119 and Reagan, *Where's the Rest of Me?,* pp. 78-79.

37. Richard Schickel, "No Method to His Madness." *Film Comment,* June 1987, pp. 11-19.

38. Wills, *Reagan's America,* p. 94.

39. Schickel, "No Method," p. 16.

40. Rogin, *Ronald Reagan,* p. 3.

41. See Wills, *Reagan's America,* p. 173 and Rogin, *Ronald Reagan,* p. 13.

42. Wills, *Reagan's America,* pp. 173 and 179.

43. Schickel, "No Method," p. 12.

44. Wills, *Reagan's America,* p. 1.

45. Jack Germond and Jules Witcover, *Blue Smoke and Mirrors* (New York: Viking Press, 1981), p. 210.

46. Wills, *Reagan's America,* p. 136.

47. "Jennings Koppel Report: Memo to the Future," transcript, p. 3.

48. Rogin, *Ronald Reagan,* p. 3.

5
Television and the Future of the U.S. Presidency

We began this study by noting that it was more concerned with the institution of the American presidency than the administration of Ronald Reagan. As Ted Koppel ponders in a television broadcast, "Somehow, it's difficult to see folks 20 to 30 years down the road being quite as mesmerized by our president as we have been. Indeed, they'll probably wonder at how readily we swallowed Ronald Reagan's many contradictions."[1] Yet, Ronald Reagan provides a blueprint for future presidents. The blueprint is one for electoral success and personal popularity but provides little insight into coalition building and policy implementation.

Although ironic, it is not surprising to presidential scholars that Reagan's second term, after a landslide victory, is one of disappointment and downright embarrassment. Historically, modern presidents have had difficulty in gaining reelection, and if reelected, maintaining popular support throughout the second term. In the early 1970s, after the shock of Johnson and the reality of Nixon, George Reedy warned of "the twilight of the presidency" when the "institution provides camouflage for all that is petty and nasty in human beings, and enables a clown or a knave to pose as Galahad and be treated with deference. . . . As a device to lead us through the stresses of modern life, it is wholly inadequate."[2] Arthur Schlesinger described the problem as one of an all-powerful, "imperial presidency." "We need a strong presidency—but a strong presidency within the constitution."[3] For James Barber, it was simply a matter of "presidential character." We need to pick "active-positive" presidents—"a presidential character who can see beyond tomorrow—and smile—[and] might yet lead us out of the wilderness."[4] For some scholars, the answer was a stronger Congress. For others it was a matter of "more" and "better" citizen participation. By 1980, however, Terry Sanford warned of the "danger of democracy," in which "we will use its name in vain, and in its name so unstructure our political institutions that nothing can be decided, or decided wisely."[5]

So what's wrong? At least with Reagan, the American people seemed happy and at least somewhat satisfied for five or six years. The fact is that our form of presidential government is in a state of transition or transformation. Television has changed the fundamental nature, structure, and function of the U.S. presidency. Reagan, by totally adapting to the medium, provides a model for analysis. The medium influences who runs, who is elected, the nature of democracy, and presidential leadership, as well as the institution itself. Although it is difficult to predict the end product, there are alarming dimensions emerging that warrant serious consideration.

WHO RUNS?

We are now at the point, Martin Schram observes, that "the instrument of television has taken control of the presidential-election process."[6] Television has taken control not in the sense of measuring candidates but as the instrument of the imagemakers. Campaigns today no longer reveal the depth of issue knowledge or understanding. Political debate is simply an exchange of predictable "sound bites." The background and experience of presidential candidates are less important than the ability to attract media support and public popularity. As professional politicians, our leaders no longer reflect the diversity of occupations and accompanying expertise of the general public. Gone are the true and mature laborers, businessmen, educators, and professionals that once comprised state and national legislatures. Television has given birth to a new type of U.S. politician and opened Washington to "outsiders."

In the future, products of the media will become the primary source of potential presidential candidates. Sports figures, movie stars, television celebrities, and political celebrities are our future leaders. Within the last few years we have witnessed the election of Clint Eastwood as mayor of Carmel and Fred Grandy (a former star of the television show *Love Boat*) as a congressman. The entertainment industry has raised money and expressed its concern over AIDS and world hunger. Rumored presidential candidates have included such people as Lee Iacocca, Bill Bradley, Bill Farley, and Walter Cronkite, to name only a few. It is very expensive to generate name recognition. Those who already have it clearly have an advantage.

The point is rather obvious. To campaign through the medium of television requires adaptation in terms of message content and delivery. As a result, we have candidates and campaigns that differ greatly from those of the non-television era.

WHO IS ELECTED?

Clearly the 1984 presidential election demonstrated that political issues and ideology matter little in selecting a president. The polls continually showed that voters favored Ronald Reagan based on elements of persona and charisma but disagreed with his issue positions. Rather than believing the public was somehow misinformed, Joan Carrigan of *NBC Nightly News* concluded "that if people were choosing Reagan even though they disagreed with him on the issues, then that must mean that issues do not matter—and so there is no need to better inform the public about them."[7]

Because of the intimate nature of television, voting for president is a personal thing—like endorsing a father or favorite aunt or uncle. It is easy to judge what we see (a very controlled image) and what we experience (i.e., television as a "hot" medium).

Americans, as already mentioned, have a rather defined set of role expectations associated with the presidency. To *be* president means to *act* like one. We want our president to be articulate, uplifting, diplomatic, even sometimes elegant, as well as to maintain a sense of humor and calmness.

John Orman's interesting book entitled *Comparing Presidential Behavior* defines and illustrates the "macho presidential style"—a style of leadership that is the product of our electoral system as well as our American myth of masculinity.[8] From the model, Orman argues that Carter's failure was largely one of not living up to the requirements of the macho style. As a result, Carter received poor media coverage and negative press. In contrast, Reagan is "the quintessential macho president" whose success is largely based upon his exercise of the macho presidential style. The macho style entails that the president be: competitive in politics and life; sports-minded and athletic; decisive, never wavering or uncertain; unemotional, never revealing true emotions or feelings; strong and aggressive, not weak or passive; powerful; and a "real man," never "feminine." It is easy to see how these elements work well on television. We remember visions of Reagan riding horses, chopping wood, taking on the Russians, bombing Libya, and surviving an assassination attempt with humor and courage.

Those who win presidential elections are those who fulfill the role expectations of the American public. And role expectations have very little to do with political issues or policies. Those who win are those who perform best on television. In discussing Reagan, Ted Koppel claims he "never fully mastered the job, but he fills the role so completely, with such grace and mastery, that we will have to wait until the footlights dim and the house lights go up again, before determining whether the play was any good at all."[9]

THE QUALITY OF DEMOCRACY AND PRESIDENTIAL LEADERSHIP

Television was once viewed as the ultimate instrument of democracy. Today, few would argue that it has increased the quantity or quality of democratic participation. Politicians use the medium to confirm rather than challenge, to present rather than to engage the public. National audiences requires generic appeals and predictable responses.

Political ritual has become political reality. We make decisions based upon superficial information and role behavior. According to Michael Rogin, Reagan's "easy slippage between movies and reality is synecdochic for a political culture increasingly impervious to distinctions between fiction and history."[10] Reagan was masterful at hiding his "backstage" behavior.[11]

Theodore Lowi argues that today we have a "plebiscitary president." "The United States," he observes, "is the one major democracy without some kind of system of collective responsibility."[12] The presidency has become the center of responsibility and national government. This leads to what Lowi characterizes as the "second republic of the United States." The "plebiscitary president" implies a ruler who governs on the basis of popular adoration. He questions the real difference between Napoleon I and Ronald Reagan. "We have a virtual cult of personality revolving around the White House."[13]

Parents have long used television to "baby-sit" children while completing work or just to keep them out of the way. In terms of governing, television functions the same way. It "baby-sits" the public. Real issues and policy dynamics are complex and unpredictable. A leader simply cannot explain and justify every action, policy, or initiative. Thus, mass leadership is one of compliance.

Television places greater importance on individualism, which emphasizes the traits of warmth, articulateness, and style, and results in personal popularity, prestige, and office legitimacy.[14] Public opinion is more important than political persuasion. Image projection is more important than policy argumentation. Jefferey Tulis charges that Reagan is a president "who often spent more of his day in photo opportunities and greeting dignitaries than in policy discussion, a president who rarely called staffers to probe or elaborate upon their very brief memos to him, a president who allegedly prepared for the Iceland summit by reading a novel."[15]

Presidential leadership today is charismatic rather than programmatic. Does this leadership style of "presidentialism" help policy formation and execution? Can the primetime presidency support tax increases, strong measures to deal with the deficit, etc.? Probably not. One of the concerns of Rogin is the "false intimacy of the modern, personified state."[16] The media encourage us to look at the president in informal contexts and allow the president to demonstrate concern for citizens. This two-way mirror contributes little to the demands of leadership, governing, or program development. We get an artificial person. We see our presidents more but know them less. As a sovereign, Thomas Hobbes warned of "the disguise or outward appearance of a man, counterfeited on the stage . . . so that a person is the same that an actor is."[17]

The office is greater than the individual. It has a life of its own. The occupants either fit the mold or must appear to fit the mold. And television is the instrument of mass production. Just as every Barbie and Ken doll is the same

in millions of households, we all see the same manufac-
tured president. The foundation of democracy is the notion
of choice. Primarily because of television, presidents and
presidential candidates will increasingly look the same,
sound the same, and, unfortunately, act the same. The
presidency has become a product and the consumers were
ready for Reagan's brand above all others.

THE PRESIDENCY AS PRODUCT

The notion that the U.S. presidency is a product available for public consumption is certainly not new. What is
new is the degree to which the office has been personalized
and separated from the daily issue and policy concerns of
the incumbent. Specific product features and attributes
are largely ignored while emphasizing generalized or even
idealized product benefits and consequences. For example,
early product advertising focused on the specific attributes
of a product. A coat would keep you warm and last a long
time. Toothpaste would clean your teeth. Today, a coat
communicates a certain style, status, or image and the
right toothpaste can make you sexy. Contemporary advertising talks about product benefits, not features. The task
simply becomes for the advertiser to find out what the user
wants from the product and then to communicate the link
between the product and the desired result. This process is
what advertisers call product positioning—positioning (or
matching) the product to the already conceived desire of
the target audience. Thus, today's advertising starts with
the minds of the consumer rather than with the attributes
of the product. Time and resources simply do not permit
the luxury of trying to convert, alter, or change already

existing attitudes or opinions. To illustrate product positioning in the most simple terms, tell me what you want a detergent to do and, guess what?, my detergent does it.

As I have argued elsewhere, the U.S. presidency, as an institution, has established a rather clear set of roles.[18] Attributes, characteristics, behavioral expectations, and restrictions are attached to all social positions. Most Americans can articulate what a president should "be" and what a president should do. The task for presidents, then, is to attempt to match their attributes and behavior (i.e., benefits) to the preconceived notions of the public. In short, the presidency, as with all commercial products, has rather specific product attributes.

The problem, however, is that these attributes are not real and do not directly correlate to the policy decisions of an administration. The expected product benefits resulting from the articulated product features seldom occur. It is like enjoying eating candy without concern for nutrition. In terms of food, being "good" is not the same as being "good for us." Presidents must affirm and reinforce the established role attributes and benefits that reduce attention to actual performance. This product positioning of the presidency partly explains why the general public can like and support Ronald Reagan while disagreeing with his policy positions.

Traditionally, product marketing concerns have focused on the "four P's": product, price, place (distribution), and promotion. In presidential elections, the nation's largest one day sale, each of these variables is important. For an incumbent president, however, the elements of product and promotion are critical.

Product

As already noted, one of the most important developments in American politics over the last ten years has been the professionalization of political communication. Undoubtedly, the king makers of contemporary politics are the new breed of political and media consultants. Once limited to the continuing cycle of campaigns, they now find themselves on the permanent staffs of elected officials. These professional politicians have become the link between electoral politics and campaigns, leaders and the public.

For the incumbent, the professional staff must maintain public excitement and support, which the president can translate to Congressional votes and program implementation. Elements of management, planning, strategy, and image creation/reinforcement are as important in governing as in campaigning.

The presidency is a product that undergoes constant evaluation, and when support sags, advertising and public relations activities are used to recapture support. Professional political communicators and pollsters, as permanent members of White House staffs, are responsible for presidents' public images. In marketing terms, they are responsible for brand identification, product life extension, and product adoption.

Promotion

Product promotion includes all forms of advertising and public relations activities. There are three trends developing:

1. Promotional activities have increased in visibility and importance for presidents, with the Reagan White House providing the blueprint for future presidents.
2. All forms and types of advertising and promotions are now being used by incumbent presidents, including paid commercials and pseudo-events, as well as targeted direct mail. Some of the more partisan efforts are sponsored by the president's party or special sympathetic groups. Nevertheless, mini-campaigns are developed to garner support for special projects and issues important to the president.
3. It has become increasingly difficult to distinguish between promotion activities and governing, information sharing and advocacy.

The best medium for product promotion is, of course, television. Television is the primary tool of and battleground for governing the nation. This implies that contemporary presidents must understand the medium to control it and possess special skills to utilize it.

The argument presented is certainly not new. The presidency is a product that is familiar to all Americans. To present a "new" and "improved" presidency is as risky and unwise as Coke's introduction of the New Coke. Americans prefer the "classic presidency"—the one in history books that possesses the values and myths of Washington, Jefferson, Lincoln, Roosevelt, and Kennedy. In many ways, to govern and maintain support, presidents must demonstrate that the product fulfills citizen expectations and has not changed. But to understand and to properly define the presidency is only part of the task. The next crucial step is to properly promote the product. To do so demands an understanding of the form and content of television.

The dangers are obvious. The presidency continues to become more symbolic. The gap between issues and personality increases. Governing becomes more of a science than an art. Skills of public performance are more important than the skills of management. Some communication colleagues may take comfort in that fact—I do not. And perhaps most importantly, the nature of political participation has changed. I am not sure that we can still characterize our form of government as democratic without changing the core definition of the word.

Finally, to show the true implications of this perspective, consider from a marketing perspective Joseph Biden's withdrawal from the Democratic presidential race of 1988 because of charges of plagiarism and fabrication of facts in public addresses. The purpose of advertising is to reduce risk in the marketplace. Marketers, therefore, develop campaigns that utilize specific appeals and language that will guarantee favorable attention and response. Few of the appeals are unique. In fact, most basic advertising texts identify a finite number of such appeals and presentation strategies and formats. Biden, as a product, wanted to reduce the risk of rejection. He wanted to gain public awareness and ultimately acceptance. There were specific appeals that historically were successful for several politicians. In recreating (in his case defining) the successful persona and hence his product, Biden utilized specific sequences of symbols that were successful in the past or in a different context (England) in evoking desired responses. Biden may be a poor politician, but he is certainly a good marketer.

CONCLUSION

Television was going to make us a more informed and democratic society. The fact is that television has not made us more informed in our electoral choices or more democratic in terms of electoral participation. And, as the Reagan presidency has demonstrated, television cannot serve as a check on presidential power. Media orchestration by an administration can dominate news coverage and presentation.

Television has contributed to the decline of political parties. Politicians can go straight to the people to build support and organization. It has increased the fragmentation of American society by becoming the instrument of special groups and causes. Television can join the "ears" of the nation but not necessarily the "hearts" of the nation. It has created a "fishbowl" government that is largely paralyzed to take decisive and reasoned actions.

It is usually at this point that one is supposed to offer brilliant insight and concrete suggestions for reform. Social analyses, however, should not always be compelled to adopt the format of a market research report or an engineer's memorandum. The processes of diagnosis and prescription are separate steps, each requiring careful preparation and analysis.

In terms of the presidency, the central question becomes how to continue to cultivate an active, democratic citizenry when those citizens have highly inflated visions of presidential grandeur and greatness. The fact is that distorted presidential perceptions lead to distorted presidential behavior. Discovering our illusions will at least serve as the first step toward discovering what our real problems are.

We need, as Martin Levin argues, to return to a "politics of institutions, not men."[19] This means a greater role and recognition of the other branches of government. Policy making is a collective affair rather than a competitive endeavor.

News needs to be a window rather than a mirror, providing more contextual stories. Perhaps more free air time will reduce the need for thirty-second art.

We also need to have a greater understanding of the role, function, and power of the media in our society. As social and scientific technology rapidly increases, we must carefully plan for their usage. As a tool, media can be used for both good and bad ends. Our task is to discern the difference.

Finally, civic responsibility and initiative should once again become a keystone of social life. Hoping presidents will alone solve critical problems is at best a risky alternative.

In 1982 I proclaimed that the institution of the American presidency was in a state of crisis.[20] The crisis, I argued, lies within the realm of the symbolic. Specifically, the crisis is the gap between the symbolic, mythic, historical presidential persona and the harsh realities and demands of today's world. The nation's mythic, heroic, and symbolic expectations of the office are no longer apropos to meet the challenges of the twenty-first century. One of the primary causes of the gap between presidential promise and performance is the mass media. Rather ironically, in an article in 1987 in *U.S. News and World Report,* Mel Elfin acknowledges that "during the past two decades, the American Presidency has become trapped between television, which exaggerates the aura of the President's power, and post-Vietnam, post-Watergate anxieties, which erode the substance of that power. In short, it is a time when Presidents are expected to do more but are given the authority to do less."[21] As the gap increases so does the disillusionment of the American public and the impotence of the presidency. The end result of the widening gap would be to make the presidency pure symbol with no referent and no substance. With the primetime presidency of Ronald Reagan, my prophecy has come true.

NOTES

1. "Jennings Koppel Report: Memo to the Future," ABC News, April 23, 1987, transcript page 13.

2. George Reedy, *The Twilight of the Presidency* (New York: The World Publishing Co., 1970), pp. xv and xvii.

3. Arthur Schlesinger, *The Imperial Presidency* (Boston: Houghton Mifflin, 1973), p. x.

4. James Barber, *The Presidential Character* (Englewood Cliffs, NJ: Prentice-Hall, 1972), p. 454.

5. Terry Sanford, *A Danger of Democracy* (Boulder, CO: Westview Press, 1981).

6. Martin Schram, *The Great American Video Game* (New York: William Morrow & Co., 1987), p. 305.

7. As noted in Schram, *Great American Video Game*, p. 289.

8. John Orman, *Comparing Presidential Behavior* (New York: Greenwood Press, 1987).

9. "Jennings Koppel Report", transcript, p. 13.

10. Michael Rogin, *Ronald Reagan, The Movie* (Beverly Hills, CA: University of California Press, 1987), p. 9.

11. See Joshua Meyrowitz, *No Sense of Place* (New York: Oxford University Press, 1985), pp. 269-279.

12. Theodore Lowi, *The Personal President* (Ithaca, NY: Cornell University Press, 1985), p. 98.

13. Lowi, *The Personal President,* p. xi.

14. Bert Rockman, *The Leadership Question* (New York: Praeger, 1984), pp. 194-199.

15. Jefferey Tulis, *The Rhetorical Presidency* (Princeton, NJ: Princeton University Press, 1987), p. 190.

16. Rogin, *Ronald Reagan,* p. 298.

17. Thomas Hobbes, *Leviathan* (New York: Macmillan, 1962), p. 125.

18. See Robert E. Denton, Jr. *The Symbolic Dimensions of the American Presidency* (Prospect Heights, IL: Waveland Press, 1982), pp. 39-57 and Robert E. Denton, Jr. and Dan Hahn, *Presidential Communication* (New York: Praeger, 1986), pp. 172-179.

19. Martin Levin, "A Call for a Politics of Institutions, Not Men" in *The Post-Imperial Presidency,* Vincent Davis, ed. (New York: Praeger, 1980), pp. 39-70.

20. Denton, *The Symbolic Dimensions of the American Presidency,* pp. 1-13, 115-129.

21. Mel Elfin, "Shrinking the Oval Office," *U.S. News and World Report,* December 7, 1987, p. 26.

Selected Bibliography

BOOKS

Altheide, David, and Snow, Robert. *Media Logic.* Beverly Hills, CA: Sage, 1979.

Aristotle. *Politics.* (Edited and translated by Ernest Barker). New York: Oxford University Press, 1970.

Arterton, Christopher. *Media Politics.* Lexington, MA: Lexington Books, 1984.

Barber, James. *The Presidential Character.* Englewood Cliffs, NJ: Prentice-Hall, 1972.

Baskerville, Barnet. *The People's Voice.* Lexington, KY: University of Kentucky Press, 1979.

Bennett, Lance. *News: The Politics of Illusion.* New York: Longman, 1983.

Blumenthal, Sidney. *The Permanent Campaign.* New York: A Touchstone Book, 1982.

Cannon, Lou. *Reagan.* New York: Putnam, 1982.

Cross, Donna. *Media-Speak.* New York: Mentor Books, 1983.

Denton, Robert E. *The Symbolic Dimensions of the American Presidency.* Prospect Heights, IL: Waveland Press, 1982.

Denton, Robert E., and Hahn, Dan. *Presidential Communication.* New York: Praeger, 1986.

Denton, Robert E., and Woodward, Gary. *Political Communication in America.* New York: Praeger, 1985.

Diamond, Edwin, and Bates, Stephen. *The Spot.* Cambridge, MA: MIT Press, 1984.

Edwards, George. *The Public Presidency.* New York: St. Martin's Press, 1983.

Erickson, Paul. *Reagan Speaks.* New York: New York University Press, 1985.

Germond, Jack, and Witcover, Jules. *Blue Smoke and Mirrors.* New York: Viking Press, 1981.

Grossman, Michael, and Kumar, Martha. *Portraying the President.* Baltimore, MD: Johns Hopkins University Press, 1981.

Hart, Roderick. *The Sound of Leadership.* Chicago: University of Chicago Press, 1987.

Hart, Roderick. *Verbal Style and the Presidency.* Orlando, FL: Academic Press, 1984.

Hobbes, Thomas. *Leviathan.* New York: Macmillan, 1962.

Innis, Harold. *The Bias of Communication,* rev. ed. Toronto, Canada: University of Toronto Press, 1964.

Innis, Harold. *Empire and Communication,* rev. ed. Toronto, Canada: University of Toronto Press, 1972.

Jamieson, Kathleen, *Packaging The Presidency.* New York: Oxford University Press, 1984.

Jamieson, Kathleen, and Campbell, Karlyn. *The Interplay of Influence.* Belmont, CA: Wadsworth, 1983.

Joslyn, Richard. *Mass Media and Elections.* Reading, MA: Addison-Wesley, 1984.

Kearns, Doris. *Lyndon Johnson and the American Dream.* New York: Harper and Row, 1976.

Kernell, Samuel. *Going Public.* Washington, D.C.: Congressional Quarterly Press, 1986.

Kessler, Frank. *The Dilemmas of Presidential Leadership.* Englewood Cliffs, NJ: Prentice-Hall, 1982.

Lowi, Theodore. *The Personal President.* Ithaca, NY: Cornell University Press, 1985.

Mast, Gerald. *A Short History of the Movies.* Indianapolis, IN: Pegasus, 1971.

Mauser, Gary. *Political Marketing*. New York: Praeger, 1983.

McLuhan, Marshall, and Fiore, Quentin. *The Medium is the Message*. New York: Bantam Books, 1967.

McLuhan, Marshall. *Understanding Media*. New York: New American Library, 1964.

Meyrowitz, Joshua. *No Sense of Place*. New York: Oxford University Press, 1985.

Nelson, Michael. *The Election of 1984*. Washington, D.C.: Congressional Quarterly Press, 1985.

Nimmo, Dan, and Combs, James. *Mediated Political Realities*. New York: Longman, 1983.

Orman, John. *Comparing Presidential Behavior*. New York: Greenwood Press, 1987.

Patterson, Thomas. *The Mass Media Election*. New York: Praeger, 1980.

Patterson, Thomas, and McClure, Robert. *The Unseeing Eye*. New York: Paragon Books, 1976.

Phillips, Kevin. *Mediacracy*. New York: Doubleday, 1974.

Pomper, Gerald; Baker, Ross; Frankovic, Kathleen; Jacob, Charles; McWilliams, Wilson; Plotkin, Henry; and Keeter, Scott. *The Election of 1984*. Chatham, NJ: Chatham House Publishers, 1985.

Reagan, Ronald, with Richard Huber. *Where's the Rest of Me?* New York: Dell Edition, 1981.

Reedy, George. *The Twilight of the Presidency*. New York: The World Publishing Co., 1970.

Reeves, Richard. *The Reagan Detour*. New York: Simon and Schuster, 1985.

Rockman, Bert. *The Leadership Question*. New York: Praeger, 1984.

Rogin, Michael. *Ronald Reagan, The Movie*. Beverly Hills, CA: University of California Press, 1987.

Rubin, Richard. *Press, Party, and Presidency*. New York: W. W. Norton, 1981.

Sanford, Terry. *A Danger of Democracy*. Boulder, CO: Westview Press, 1981.

Schlesinger, Arthur. *The Imperial Presidency*. Boston: Houghton Mifflin, 1973.

Schram, Martin. *The Great American Video Game.* New York: William Morrow & Co., 1987.
Schwartz, Tony. *The Responsive Chord.* New York: Anchor Books, 1973.
Spragens, William. *The Presidency and the Mass Media in the Age of Television.* Lanham, MD: University Press of America, 1979.
Tulis, Jefferey. *The Rhetorical Presidency.* Princeton, NJ: Princeton University Press, 1987.
Wayne, Stephen. *The Road to the White House,* 2nd ed. New York: St. Martin's Press, 1984.
Weaver, David, Graber, Doris, McCombs, Maxwell, and Eyal, Chaim. *Media Agenda-Setting in Presidential Elections.* New York: Praeger, 1981.
Wills, Garry. *Reagan's America.* New York: Doubleday, 1987.

ARTICLES

Adams, William. "Media Power in Presidential Elections." *The President and the Public.* Doris Graber, ed. Philadelphia, PA: Institute for Study of Human Issues, 1982.
Becker, Samuel. "Rhetorical Studies for the Contemporary World." *The Prospect for Rhetoric.* Lloyd Bitzer and Edwin Black, eds. Englewood Cliffs, NJ: Prentice-Hall, 1971.
Carson, Tom. "The Prime Time of Ronald Reagan." *Voice.* September 4, 1984, pp. 14-15.
Elfin, Mel. "Shrinking the Oval Office." *U.S. News and World Report.* December 7, 1987, pp. 26-29.
Graber, Doris. "Introduction: Perspectives on Presidential Linkage." *The President and the Public.* Doris Graber, ed. Philadelphia, PA: Institute for Study of Human Issues, 1982.
Hart, Roderick; Jerome, Patrick; and McComb, Karen. "Rhetorical Features of Newscasts About the President." *Critical Studies in Mass Communication,* vol. 1, no. 3. September 1984, pp. 261-284.
Iyenzar, Shanto, and Kinder, Donald. "Psychological Accounts

of Agenda-Setting." *Mass Media and Political Thought.* Sidney Kraus and Richard Perloff, eds. Beverly Hills, CA: Sage, 1985.

"Jennings Koppel Report: Memo to the Future." ABC News. April 23, 1987. Transcript.

Joslyn, Richard. "Political Advertising and the Meaning of Elections." *New Perspectives on Political Advertising.* Lynda Kaid, et al., eds. Carbondale, IL: Southern Illinois University Press, 1986.

Kaid, Lynda, and Davidson, Dorothy. "Elements of Videostyle." *New Perspectives on Political Advertising.* Lynda Kaid, et al., eds. Carbondale, IL: Southern Illinois University Press, 1986.

Lasswell, Harold. "The Structure and Function of Communication in Society." *The Communication of Ideas.* Lyman Bryson, ed. New York: Institute of Religious and Social Studies, 1948.

Levin, Martin. "A Call for a Politics of Institutions, Not Men." *The Post-Imperial Presidency.* Vincent Davis, ed. New York: Praeger, 1980.

Manheim, Jorol. "Can Democracy Survive Television?" *Media Power in Politics.* Doris Graber, ed. Washington, D.C.: Congressional Quarterly, Inc., 1984.

Mathews, Donald. "The News Media and the 1976 Presidential Nominations." *Race for the Presidency.* James David Barber, ed. Englewood Cliffs, NJ: Prentice-Hall, 1978.

McQuail, Dennis. "The Influence and Effects of Mass Media." *Media Power in Politics.* Doris Graber, ed. Washington, D.C.: Congressional Quarterly Inc., 1984.

Miller, Arthur; Wattenberg, Martin; and Malanchuk, Oksana. "Cognitive Representations of Candidate Assessments." *Political Communication Yearbook 1984.* Keith Sanders, Lynda Kaid, and Dan Nimmo, eds. Carbondale, IL: Southern Illinois University Press, 1985.

Patterson, Thomas, and Davis, Richard. "The Media Campaign: Struggle for the Agenda." *The Election of 1984.* Michael Nelson, ed. Washington, DC: Congressional Quarterly Press, 1985.

"Playboy Interview: Marshall McLuhan." *Playboy Magazine.*
    March, 1969, pp. 51-74.
Schickel, Richard. "No Method to His Madness." *Film Comment.*
    June, 1987, pp. 11-19.
Streitmatter, Rodger. "The Impact of Presidential Personality
    on News Coverage in Major Newspapers." *Journalism
    Quarterly.* Spring, 1985, pp. 66-73.

Index

ABOUT THE AUTHOR

ROBERT E. DENTON, JR. has degrees in political science and communication from Wake Forest University and Purdue University. He teaches and writes in the areas of the American presidency, political communication, mass media, advertising, and contemporary rhetorical theory. Denton is the author of a book on the presidency and co-author of books on social movements, persuasion in contemporary American life, political communication, and presidential communication (the latter two also with Praeger). In addition, he has published articles in the fields of political science, advertising, and communication. He is currently head of the Department of Communication Studies at Virginia Polytechnic Institute and State University.